CW00469130

THE ART OF NOTE TAKING

YOUR RESEARCH-BASED GUIDE TO TAKING NOTES
THAT WILL STICK TO YOUR MEMORY

THINKNETIC

CONTENTS

GET 3 FREE BONUSES!

Free Bonus #1

Our Bestseller *Critical Thinking In A Nutshell*

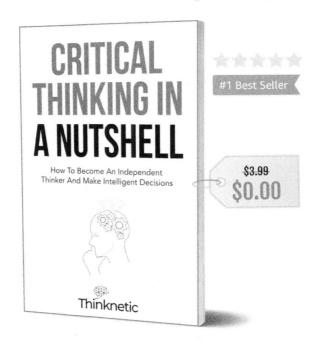

Did You Know That 93% Of CEOs Agree That This Skill Is More Important Than Your College Degree?

Here's just a fraction of what you'll discover inside:

- How to shortcut the famous Malcom Gladwell "10,000 Hours Rule" to become an expert critical thinker, fast
- What a WW2 pilot and the people of Romania can teach you about critical thinking - this is the KEY to not making huge mistakes
- Actionable, easy exercises to drill home every point covered in the novel. You won't "read and forget" this book

"This book is a good primer for the beginner and a good refresh for the expert who wants to bring more critical thinking into their problem-solving. Easy to read and understand, buy this book."

(Kevin on April 19, 2021)

"This book is unlike any other on Critical Thinking. The author puts an entirely new twist in critical thinking. Very easy to understand. Give it a read and see for yourself."

(Knowledge Seeker on April 16, 2021)

"The explanations are straight forward, sensible and usable with some interesting ideas about how this can be taught or learned."

(Dave Crisp on April 14, 2021)

Free Bonus #2
Thinking Cheat Sheet *Break Your Thinking Patterns*

Free Bonus #3
Thinking Guide *Flex Your Wisdom Muscle*

A glimpse into what you'll discover inside:

- If your thinking is flawed and what it takes to fix it (the solutions are included)
- Simple and effective strategies to make sound and regret-free decisions
- Tried and true hacks to elevate your rationality and change your live for the better
- Enlightening principles to guide your thoughts and actions (gathered from the wisest man of all time)

Go to thinknetic.net to download for free!

(Or simply scan the code with your camera)

INTRODUCTION

Charles was in fifth grade when he came home in a bad mood. "Mom, aren't you friends with Mike's mom? Can you talk to her?" he said with a scowl. I asked him what the matter was. "Mike always keeps borrowing my notebooks. He doesn't write his own notes. He copies from me. But I need to review my notes because we might have a test the next day." I assured him I would have a talk with her.

Then, Nikki, his sister in the sixth grade, breezed in and went straight to her favorite video game. I called out to her, "Young lady, shouldn't you be doing your homework?" "No homework today, Mom," she dismissively said. I took her notebooks from her schoolbag, opened them one by one, and stared at empty pages where her notes for the day should have been. "Didn't you have lessons today? Where are your notes?" She nonchalantly answered, "No worries. I'll copy from Alyssa's notebook tomorrow."

Growing up, all of us have been there. Writing notes in class is probably what most of us associate with our school days. It's not an exaggeration to say that we probably spent 80% of our time in class – not counting physical education and music – writing what the teacher dictates or writes on the blackboard.

And it's a tedious task. I remember shaking my hand and stretching my cramped fingers after hours of relentless scribbling. At the time, it seemed a senseless, mechanical task that elementary school teachers made us do. In high school and college, the teachers left note-taking pretty much to their students' volition. At first, it felt like being set free, but later we discover it's much like a catch-22. Lazy to take notes? That's OK. You'll pay for it when you get a failing grade on your tests. To pass, you need to pay attention in class and take notes.

In the chapters following, you will discover five of the most popular and productive note-taking methods. These are the outline, mind mapping, sentence, charting, and Cornell methods. They are only a few of the many techniques students can use to take notes to help them get better grades. Each chapter focuses on one of the methods and systematically provides a definition and description for it. It will walk you through the instructions for performing the method and identifies the situations where it is best applied. Examples of each method will give you a practical feel for it. Finally, there is an exercise and summary before we segue to the next chapter.

We are particularly elated to include the final chapter in this book. Other references on note-taking methods focus only on the processes of recording information. More than merely synthesizing techniques in note-taking, it is a discourse of how both students and lecturers may cooperate to improve knowledge transfer, based on empirical research on note-taking. We practitioners may have instinctively developed a sense of how to deliver a lecture in a way that encourages our students to take quality notes, but this comes only after decades of lecturing. The time and opportunity for students to learn these methods are even more transient. This chapter encapsulates the most effective insights and instructions that both students and teachers can immediately put into practice.

Ultimately, the goal of note-taking mastery is to enhance learning – better grades are only a happy by-product. Therefore, we precede the discussion of note-taking with a chapter that explores our learning styles and strategies. You will likely find this chapter useful in gaining insights into the different ways we capture, process, and organize information. By acquiring an understanding of how we learn, we acquire the ability to identify obstacles to our learning and how we may eliminate these obstacles to improve the way we learn.

While the topics in this book appear geared more toward classroom application, the techniques you will encounter here are useful in our daily personal and work activities. We take notes during office meetings, client conferences, professional training sessions, and seminars. We write in our journals or diaries, make grocery lists, and take notes on anything of interest, from recipes to golf tips to investments. We constantly learn and expand our knowledge, and for every new thing we learn, we realize untold present and future benefits from noting it down.

It is my pleasure to share with you the insights and experiences I have gained as a lifetime student and teacher. I completed courses in engineering, finance, business administration, and law – widely divergent fields of study that helped me understand and employ different types of learning styles. I had also taught for four decades in these fields, where I came to appreciate the subtleties of conveying information to students and trainees from the academe to the workplace. As an honor student, I have also been fortunate to discover the manner and approach to learning success and find joy in sharing them with others and you.

Before we embark on this journey together, let us remember that note-taking is not an end in itself. Oftentimes, it is the beginning of something bigger and better than anything we could have anticipated. Tony Kushner is an American award-winning author, playwright, and screenwriter. He is a Pulitzer Prize recipient and has twice won the Tony Award for his body of work. Prolific writers like Kushner are worthy of our admiration and praise. They also make us wonder how they could produce a string of excellent works while most of us cannot even come up with one. Kushner hints at his secret in this quote:

"One of the things I love about my job as a playwright or as a screenwriter is that I get to do a lot of research and a lot of thinking and taking a lot of notes before I turn it in."– Tony Kushner [1]

As this quote suggests, taking notes can be instrumental in our success. Taking quality notes will go a long way toward ensuring it. The chapters we are about to journey through will doubtless equip us with the tools to become quality note-takers.

Let us turn the page and begin.

Dianna Gene P. Aquino

For Ar and Lily

1

WHY TAKE NOTES?

And so, my dear brownies, don't forget to bring a tickler with you wherever we go. It will be your most important tool; mark my words.

As a grade-three girl scout, I hung onto every word of our troop leader as we prepared for our camping trip. That was the first time I heard the word "tickler." The image of a feather gently stroking the underside of a foot quickly came to mind. Our troop leader probably got the impression that her words flew over our heads, so she clarified: "Tickler. It's a small notebook you can handily carry around." Aha, so that's it...

In the 50 years since then, the tickler habit stuck with me for no other reason than its innate usefulness. To this day, I always keep a little notepad in a purse or pocket, with a short-stubbed pencil inserted into its spine. Through the years, many things went into my ticklers. You could usually tell my pursuits of the moment based on the notes I jotted down. Homework to be done. Projects to complete. Appointments to keep. Grocery items to grab. PTA meetings to attend. Stocks to recommend. Legal articles to memorize. Requirements to fulfill for Canadian residency. Items to record hurriedly to "tickle" the memory and spur recollection at a later time.

Early on, I discovered that some of the notes I wrote down were more useful than others. The length was unimportant; some single-word notes proved very useful. Other notes, although supported by contextual data, were later incomprehensible to me. For instance:

"Alistair DL, 5191994, CHDL"

Feeling secure that I had preserved the data, I quickly pushed it out of my mind to attend to more pressing matters. I only happened to revisit it six weeks later when I rifled through my tickler. Who was Alistair? Was this a date? And what is the four-letter code? A year passed before I drove through an infrequently traversed street and glanced at a shop sign. Of course, Alistair Distinction Lamps, contact number 519-1994, chandelier. I was supposed to call them to canvass the price of their chandelier. But for all the information it contained, the note meant nothing to me when I saw it, preventing me from using it to my advantage.

The Importance Of Note-Taking

We may not have realized it at the time, but effective note-taking has many important uses:[1]

1. It Aids Our Memory.

We take notes to remember things. Ever wonder why we studied the multiplication table over several grade levels in elementary? It's because of the "spacing effect." To make lessons stick in our minds, we need to revisit them several times to remember them in the long term. By keeping notes, we can more frequently review the ideas and information we want to remember well into the future.

2. It Helps Us Learn And Understand Better.

When we first encounter ideas through listening or reading, we rarely truly understand them. Listening and visually scanning words are passive processes. Understanding requires actively mulling over what was heard or read; often, we refer to this as "digesting" the information. When we write down what we hear or read, such as in a classroom setting, then we engage in an active process. Taking notes involves thinking about the ideas encountered, choosing the words to write, and assembling your own statements, phrases, or diagrams. Notes are the concepts we formulate and assimilate for ourselves.

3. It Keeps Us Awake.

While I was a student, I thought that short catnaps during long, boring lectures would escape the attention of the teacher who stood on the platform in front of the class. When I became a teacher, I discovered how wildly erroneous that presumption had been. Standing elevated above the students' eye level, I could see every half-closed eyelid and nodding head, even the occasional drool. I also noticed that those who kept awake were actively scrolling away at their notes, while their soporific classmates seemed frozen and inanimate.

When we take notes, not only do we write, but we also think. This mental-physical activity keeps our brain alert and our hands and eyes constantly moving, preventing us from being lulled to sleep by the lecture. Students cannot always have a lively teacher, but they do have to earn their grades by learning the lesson. Taking notes is the best activity they could do while seated for hours.

4. It Provides A Repository And Documentation Of Our Thinking.

In 1977, I was one of the first high school students to earn a government scholarship for a computer programming course. Computers then were large, clunky machines that filled an entire room. We encoded our programs in punch cards (i.e., cards with holes punched into them) which we fed to a large machine called a card reader. We then waited for 30 minutes while the central processing unit, another large machine, ran our program and processed the data that we included. We then get a large piece of paper containing the results from the printer, another large machine. We had no keyboards, screens, monitors, or speakers. All the information was in electronic binary digits, so if not for the printout, we had no record at all that any data had been processed.

Much like the computer's electronic pulses, our thoughts are abstract and perishable, therefore prone to disappear over time. Notes are the "printouts" of our thinking process. When we take notes, we give our thoughts a physical form that is tangible and permanent. As we learn and add new things to this collection, we reconcile what we know now with what we knew then. Notes are the records of our thoughts that we may accumulate and revisit again and again.

5. It Serves As A Good Resource For Our Writing.

Notes do not exist only for us to collect thoughts with; they also provide us with fresh ideas when we write. Notes enable us to interpret, synthesize, and create our own concepts. They become the wellspring from which we compose our contribution to the written knowledge pool.

Some students are naturally good at note-taking, while others struggle before finding their own style. Note-taking is a personal activity; no two students have the same notes. It is likely that many students simply do not get to realize the need to develop good note-taking skills and thereby miss this golden opportunity.

The Usefulness Of Note-Taking

Does note-taking produce tangible results, like better academic performance and higher grades? Academic research appears to back up this hypothesis. Here are but a few of them.

- Note-taking among secondary students significantly correlates with students' academic performance, and the effect is magnified when note-taking is combined with good study habits. Note-taking has a higher magnitude of contribution than study habits. [2]
- The same phenomenon among university students learning English as a Foreign Language (EFL) in Jordan. Strategic note-taking significantly improves EFL learners' academic performance and is a strong predictor of the learners' academic performance. [3]
- Note-taking improves students' recall of instructional material and understanding of its content. It also assists students in preparing for examinations. Note-taking improves students' overall grades. [4]

But of course, good classroom performance and higher grades are only the external manifestations of internal mental processes. The decline in students' ability to take notes effectively is influenced by the educational system's lack of emphasis on critical thinking development and the formation of fundamental learning habits, including listening, reading, and writing.

Shortcomings Of Our Educational System

The Education System Does Not Encourage Critical Thinking.

Ruggiero described critical thinking as "the art of thinking about thinking" [5] with the intent to improve our thinking. People who have mastered the art of critical thinking can embrace and take charge of their own learning. Students who are critical thinkers approach their lessons in "a more thoughtful and effective manner, ask more challenging questions, and participate in the learning process more intensely." [6]

Thinking is done consciously or subconsciously. It is "searching for answers while reaching for meaning." [7]When we learn to think critically, we not only absorb stimuli from our environment, but we endow them with our interpretation of their significance. Critical thinking is a sense-making process. Unfortunately, while educators and politicians have stressed for the past 50 years the importance of providing students with critical thinking skills, little has been done to achieve this. Seventy-five percent of employers in the United States claim that the students they hire after 12 or more years of formal education cannot think critically and solve problems. [8]

· · ·

The Education System Does Not Promote Good Writing.

There is a difference between teaching students how to do something and encouraging them to do something well. The former is technical; the latter is motivational. Mastering the technical becomes a habit we could perform mechanically, but gaining the right motivation enables us to perform the activity skillfully and optimally.

Teachers must not only teach students critical thinking skills in the classroom. They must also provide them opportunities to put these skills to use. Most importantly, teachers must also inspire them to continue practicing those skills independently when they leave the classroom. 9

Pre-Lecture Preparation

If you anticipate taking notes during a scheduled event, such as a lecture, you will have a more rewarding note-taking experience if you prepare beforehand. This means equipping yourself with enough paper and a pen that will not run out of ink. Or, you should fully charge your laptop or other electronic device and prepare a power bank in case the lecture goes over time.

More important than the material preparations are the mental preparations for the event. Read on the topic ahead of time. Critical thinking that yields good notes requires understanding the basic knowledge on which the lecture is built. If possible, ask in advance for a lecture outline or topics on which the speaker will expound.

These will help you understand the context of the lecture and allow you to formulate incisive questions to ask the speaker. It helps to get a notion of the lecturer's style beforehand. You will be better able to organize your notes according to his presentation.

Action Steps

As you go through this book, you'll see "Action Steps" at the end of each chapter. These are practical suggestions aimed at realizing some concrete benefit out of our discussion. For this first chapter, try this simple "action plan."

1. Get yourself a "tickler." It could be any small notebook with a writing instrument such as a small pencil or pen. Those who prefer an e-notepad may use the note app on their cellphones. If you are like me, you might not have used this app before or even realized it existed.

2. As you go through your day, be conscious of your thoughts during those "passive" activities, such as commuting to school or work or waiting for your ride. Maybe you recall something while watching a movie or show.

3. Pen and tickler (or electronic device) in hand, quickly write down what you have been thinking. It could be in a shorthand mode with which you are comfortable. For instance: "Supper tonight – steak and potatoes." Or, "Call Mom. I haven't called her in a month. It's her birthday tomorrow." Or some such thing that crosses your mind.

4. Don't stick with sentences or phrases. Doodle if you are so inclined. Write down the things that strike you, which you normally commit to memory and then forget anyway. Watching Peaky Blinders Season 1 on Netflix, I was struck by Thomas Shelby's whisper, "In the Bleak Midwinter," which reminded me of a beloved Christmas carol. I made a mental note of it, then quickly forgot it. Luckily, a choir sang the song in Season 3. I jumped, "That's it!" and wrote it down on a napkin. Good thing I did not throw it away by mistake. When my sons asked for suggestions for their choir's Christmas repertoire, I gave them the napkin. Their rendition on Christmas Eve Mass was heavenly!

5. Every so often, go through the notes on the tickler or device. A physical notebook may get old and battered, but keep using the same tickler until the pages are full and you need a new one. Through the years, I have found great joy and comfort in going through those personal notes, not to mention functionality. I hope you will likewise be pleasantly surprised!

Moving On

Jotting down notes as a formal school or work activity or merely recalling grocery items for the home is something we will likely do all our lives. We should therefore adopt the right habits for note-taking to serve our purposes. The next chapter will give us a bird's eye view of different note-taking methods we will find useful for different needs and learning styles associated with our choice of methods.

Key Takeaways

- Taking notes is important to aid our memory, learning, and understanding. Our notes are a vital repository and documentation of our thinking and serve as a good source for future writing.
- Effective note-taking helps students perform better academically and is an excellent tool to complement good study habits. It also significantly improves the learning capabilities of students for whom English is a second language.
- Students who are taught to think critically excel at note-taking because they approach the lesson more thoughtfully and intensively.
- Note-taking is a requisite and a by-product of effective learning. More importantly than teaching students note-taking techniques, teachers should motivate them to engage more actively in the learning process.

2

LEARNING STYLES AND NOTE-TAKING METHODS

How we learn [1]

Teresa was my classmate in law school. Brilliant student, she earned a summa-cum-laude with her Bachelor of Arts in Philosophy degree in college. She was captain of the debate team and was at the threshold of a wonderful career as a strategist in a world-renowned think tank. We began our law studies together and luckily made it through the tough freshman year. Halfway through our sophomore courses, I found her in the restroom weeping inconsolably.

"I am flunking civil law," she said when I asked her what the problem was. "Pffft! Not you, little Miss Genius!" I said. "No, it's true. Dean Pearce finally lost his patience with me because I would not answer his question the way he wanted. You know me. I always answer according to my understanding of the lesson, in my own words, the way I visualize the essence of the question. But no, he kept shouting: 'What are you saying? Does the law say that? Tell me what the law says, word for word!' I tried to argue, but he threw me out of class. He said there's no way I could become a lawyer because I don't think like one!"

It struck me that Teresa was right. Our venerable dean was a stickler for memorization, to the last comma and semicolon. He believed that quoting the letter of the law was key to its understanding. But Teresa learned by creating pictures in her head. When we studied legal cases, she saw the petitioner, the respondent, the legal controversy, their lawyers' arguments, and the judge deciding the issue. She then interpreted how the law was applied based on the situation. Some professors acknowledge the merits of that learning style as providing a deep understanding of the legal principle. The dean was not one of them.

The following semester, Teresa quit the course. I hoped she found another school that aligned better with her learning style and continued her law studies. She would have made an excellent lawyer.

Four Core Learning Styles – Neil Fleming's VARK Model

We each have our learning styles. Scholarly studies have differentiated learning styles through the years, but the most fundamental and widely accepted of these classifications is the VARK model. VARK stands for the four common learning styles – visual, auditory, reading and writing, and kinesthetic. Fleming and Mills first developed the theory of the four learning modalities in 1992.[2] In general, they refer to the method of learning by which an individual better retains information learned. To some extent, the particular method is linked to the individual's preference and capability to learn. It also relates to the type of information the individual seeks to learn.

Visual (Spatial)

Visual learners are better predisposed to remember information in graphic form. They absorb information better that is rendered in picture forms such as diagrams, figures, symbols, charts, arrows, and similar other artifacts. Rather than talk and act, they observe better and are usually more detail-oriented than other learners. They may struggle with directions that are delivered only through spoken words.

Auditory (Aural)

Auditory listeners tend to learn more effectively if sound accompanies the lesson. These are the types of students who retain more information through listening rather than reading. They respond better to a lecture, particularly when they can restate or repeat the new ideas in their own words. They also learn more when they discuss the lesson in a conversational manner, such as in a question-and-answer forum.

Reading And Writing (Verbal)

As the name suggests, reading/writing learners prefer to learn through written words. There is some overlap between reading/writing and visual learners because the written word is visual. The verbal learning method, which the reading/writing style has evolved to, now includes listening and speaking. Note that this also overlaps with the auditory or aural method in so far as the sound listened to are spoken words. [3]

Kinesthetic (Physical)

The kinesthetic method, also known as the physical learning style, best adheres to the "hands-on" approach – i.e., learning by doing. It caters to learners with a strong preference for information conveyed through the senses, case studies, practical examples, trial and error, demonstrations, and the like. [4] The main elements in kinesthetic learning are active movement and experience.

Kinesthetic learners are most productive when their five senses are engaged in an activity that shows how the principles work in real-world situations.[5] Kinesthetic learners are also known as tactile learners in so far as they process information effectively using their bodies and doing something.[6]

Other Learning Strategies

In addition to the VARK (visual, auditory, read/write or verbal, and kinesthetic or physical learning styles), researchers and theorists have added three more to make the list more exhaustive. These are the *logical, social,* and *solitary* learning methods.

Logical (Mathematical)

Some learners rely more on logic and reasoning in retaining information. This type of learning also includes solving problems with numbers or mathematical learning. Logical learning effectively analyzes cause and effect relationships.

Social (Interpersonal)

Social learners process information best by relating and interacting with other people. They communicate well with people both verbally and non-verbally and are frequently strong leaders. If you are a social learner, other people tend to instinctively approach you to ask for advice and listen to what you have to say. On your part, you have a talent for empathizing with them, sensing what they have to say, how they feel, and what motivates them. [7]

Solitary (Intrapersonal)

A solitary learner absorbs and retains information better by focusing on their thoughts and feelings in private. If other people distract you easily and you prefer to study and research alone, then you are a solitary learner. Many people who learn introspectively later augment what they have learned using the other six methods.[8]

The first five of these seven learning styles are highly descriptive about what form the data we learn takes. We prefer learning information embodied in particular forms, such as pictures, sounds, words, numbers, and movement. The last two are more descriptive of the setting we prefer to learn in, by ourselves or with others. I remember how my law classmates preferred to form study groups, bouncing off ideas among each other and getting more insights that way. Others cannot stand the din and prefer to lock themselves up in a quiet room to "hear themselves think." Sounds familiar?

Approaches To Organizing And Processing Ideas

Aside from the VARK model and its expanded version, other categories of learning styles give us fresh insights into how we organize and process new ideas. David Kolb's Learning Styles Model is one theory that has become very popular among educators, academics, managers, and trainers since its introduction in 1984.

Kolb's theory deals less with the form of the information absorbed but more with how it is absorbed. Kolb states that we acquire new knowledge from gaining new experiences. Check out the following figure, which is dubbed the Experiential Learning Cycle. We undergo four stages when we learn – feeling, watching, thinking, and doing.

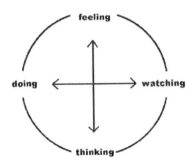

Kolb's four-stage learning cycle [9]

Kolb gave these stages unique terms:

Concrete Experience (Feeling)

This refers to the new experience we encounter or a new interpretation of a previously encountered experience. For instance, a child goes with her father to the candy store. The father gives his daughter two coins and tells her to give them to the lady at the counter. She does, and the lady takes the money and gives her a candy bar in return.

Reflective Observation (Watching)

This is the new perception or phenomenon we recognize as important or inconsistent with our previous experience. In our example, the child observed that the two coins marked "5 cents" were the equivalent of a candy bar labeled "10 cents" on the store shelf. She observes as the lady exchanges the candy for the money.

Abstract Conceptualization (Thinking)

Abstract conceptualization refers to the new idea that our observation gives rise to. Alternatively, it could also pertain to the change in our previous understanding as a result of the observation. The child, who learned in school the mathematical concept that "5 + 5 = 10," associates the two nickels with the candy worth 10 cents. She realizes that her school lesson has a meaning she can apply in real life.

Active Experimentation (Doing)

This is the practical application of the new idea learned. The child now knows that even without her father, she can present two nickels to buy a ten-cent item. Or, by extension, she can present a dime to buy the same item or two dimes to buy two of them.

I was five years old when my father picked me up from kindergarten class and brought me to the store across the street. I remember the experience well because realizing that school lessons are useful in real life hit me like a "eureka" moment. I learned the concept of "value" and that money was equivalent to things of the same value.

Is there a particular order to the four stages of learning? Although the example appears to follow a sequence, in contemplating the learning process, there doesn't seem to be a particular sequence. Any two stages along different continuums could happen simultaneously and even repetitively. We watch, feel, think, and do things spontaneously when we learn.

The figure below is an expanded version of Kolb's four stages of learning. We still see the four actions and the special terms assigned to them by Kolb, but we see other elements. The horizontal arrows are called the "processing continuum" because watching and doing are the physical activities we perform – how we approach a task. The vertical arrows are called the "perception continuum" because they are the mental and emotional responses to what we learn.

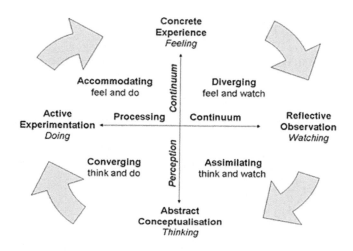

Kolb's learning styles [10]

The arrows in the diagram dissect the circle into four quadrants. Each quadrant combines two of the four stages of learning, one stage from each of the continuums. According to Kolb, we cannot equally perform the variables on a single axis at the same time. For instance, we cannot do and watch or feel and think simultaneously and to the same degree. Our individual learning styles result from these two decisions – think or feel, do or watch.

Thus, Kolb defines four learning styles according to the combination of possible responses.

1. *Diverging* is the combination of concrete experience (feeling) and reflective observation (watching).

People who are predisposed to feeling and watching are sensitive and capable of viewing concrete situations from different perspectives. Their preference for watching rather than doing inclines them towards gathering information and employing their imagination to solve problems. This style seeks to generate new ideas; thus, it is "diverging." If you are imaginative, emotional, prefer to work in groups, and can accept other people's ideas with an open mind, then you likely are a diverging learner.

An example of learning through diverging is brainstorming. Individuals form a group and try to solve a problem by coming up with as many new ideas as they can imagine. Explorers and anthropologists are learners who typically engage in diverging. The subject matter of diverging learners is mostly associated with people, culture, history, and the arts.

2. *Assimilating* is the combination of abstract conceptualization (thinking) and reflective observation (watching).

Combining watching and thinking pertains to the learning style called assimilating. This style emphasizes observing the facts and applying reasoning to understand their meaning. Learners best at assimilating typically observe abstract situations and use logic to formulate theories. They are more interested in ideas and concepts than people or things with practical value. They also mostly work independently rather than in groups.

This type of learning is called "assimilating" because it draws together varied observations and arrives at a general theory. It is most effective in science careers that deal with primary research (compared to practical development). Assimilating is most fitting in theoretical fields such as philosophy, mathematics, information technology, and science.

3. *Converging* is the combination of abstract conceptualization (thinking) and active experimentation (doing).

This learning style is for people who prefer watching and therefore possess the knack for gathering information from various sources in their environment. They logically process this data to arrive at actionable solutions to problems. The converging style of learning best addresses practical issues and technical tasks. It is not as applicable in problems related to people and interpersonal relations.

If assimilating relates to pure theory and research, converging relates to practical application and development. For instance, physicists explore theories regarding the matter (i.e., assimilating), while engineers apply these theories to designs for machines and devices for our use (i.e., converging). Biological researchers perform original research on new molecules and compounds (assimilating). Their discoveries become the basis for developing new drugs by pharmaceutical researchers (converging).

. . .

4. *Accommodating* is the combination of concrete experience (feeling) and active experimentation (doing).

People inclined towards accommodating techniques employ feeling or empathy and therefore work best with issues related to people and the social sciences. They also enjoy adopting a hands-on approach to practical situations. Learners using this style seek new challenges and experiences, act on gut instinct and intuition rather than logic, and rely more on the analysis of others rather than their own. The majority of the population makes use of the accommodating learning style. [11]

David and Alice Kolb linked the Kolb learning styles with the five levels of behavior. The following table summarizes previous research that has identified how learning styles are determined at these different levels.

Behavior level	Diverging	Assimilating	Converging	Accommodating
Personality types	Introverted Feeling	Introverted Intuition	Extraverted Thinking	Extraverted Sensation
Educational specialization	Arts, English History Psychology	Mathematics Physical Science	Engineering Medicine	Education Communication Nursing
Professional career	Social service Arts	Sciences Research Information	Engineering Medicine Technology	Sales Social service Education
Current jobs	Personal jobs	Information jobs	Technical jobs	Executive jobs
Adaptive competencies	Valuing skills	Thinking skills	Decision skills	Action skills

Much as the vast literature on learning styles indicates that this theory is widely accepted, let us also remember that some scholars regard learning styles as a myth. They disagree that students learn faster or better if their teachers adopt a style that matches their preferred learning modality. [13]But proving whether pedagogy provides better results when matched with learning preferences is not our present concern.

We discuss here the varied ways people learn and their preferences for certain styles, because how they gather information affects the way they resolve these into notes that best work for them. We all know that some of us understand and work well with mathematical equations, while others are lost when they are confronted by numbers and symbols. By the same token, some of us find great enjoyment in reading a novel, while others would prefer to watch the movie version. When we take notes, some will remember more if they draw a picture rather than write a paragraph. It helps to understand the way we absorb information in its different forms.

Before we can start taking organized notes, we should also have some idea about how to compress the lessons we have learned into concise and comprehensible blocks of written texts. We should know how to summarize.

Summarizing

Summarizing is creating a concise version of a selection or article that embodies its main ideas. Typically, we summarize for three reasons: to comply with an assignment to show we understand the selection, to keep notes that will serve as a memory aid, or to create an overview of other researchers' studies as part of a literature review.

There are five important steps in creating a written summary. [14]

Step 1: Read The Text.

Reading here does not simply mean going through the words. To read with understanding, you need to do three things. First, do a preliminary scan. This will give you an idea of the length of the text and how it is organized into subtopics. Second, return to the beginning and read the text more carefully, highlighting important ideas as you come across them. Lastly, skim through the text one more time to confirm that you understand it. This will be a good time to review difficult passages and statements to have a second look and maybe a second opinion of them.

Step 2: Break The Text Down Into Sections.

Essentially, in this step, you will be analyzing the text. Merriam-Webster defines "analyze" as "separating or distinguishing the parts of something" to discover its true meaning or inner relationships.[15] You will essentially break down and dissect the text you are summarizing. If the text has subtitles, use these subtitles as the guide to identifying the sections. The subtitles give a clue about the key points of the text. If there are no subtitles, search for the topic sentences of succeeding paragraphs. If a group of paragraphs discusses a particular thought or group of ideas, then you can identify this group as a section.

Breaking down the text into segments or sections makes the task of summarizing easier and more systematic. Rather than looking at the text as a monolith, focusing on each section at a time will effectively conserve your efforts to yield clearer insights into the key points.

Step 3: Identify The Key Points In Each Section.

Portions of the text you had recognized as sections have something in common – they exhibit a unity of thought or concept. Otherwise, you would not have grouped them into a section. Your task now is to identify the main idea the section conveys and the key points that it discusses in support of the main idea. If you feel that this is a further dissection or breaking down, you are right. In fact, the larger the text you are summarizing, the more levels of analysis you will be carrying out. Eventually, you will arrive at key points that you can no longer break down. These are the important ideas you must gather and incorporate into the summary.

. . .

Step 4: Write Down The Key Points With The Pertinent Explanations.

Let's say you have segmentized the text into sections and the sections into key concepts you feel are vital to recall. Essentially, you have arrived at your summary, but it is still in your head. You must now immortalize this summary in written form so that a few days or weeks into the future, when you would have forgotten it, it is still in a form that you may retrieve and reread. When writing down the key points, remember to qualify them with supporting explanations. There is no requisite to jot down a novel word or phrase if its essential meaning or context is not also preserved. However, do not hesitate to discard thoughts that you feel lose their relevance upon review.

When writing down the key points, observe the levels through which you broke them down, from the main topic to a section, to a subsection--and so forth. This organization of ideas will be invaluable in reconstructing the hierarchy of thought and relationships of concepts conveyed in the text. It will also help you construct a relevant mental model that you can apply in future analogous real-world situations.

Step 5: Check The Summary Against The Article.

The final check should not be discounted. Ensure that your sections and key points align with those of the original article. Also, remember that your summary necessarily embodies your own words, except for important quotes that should acknowledge the original author. Therefore, compare the text of the summary to the article. Are there inadvertently "plagiarized" phrases? Have the proper citations been made?

We now understand the modes of learning and how they relate to the learner and the material being learned. We also have an idea about how to compress the lesson effectively through summarizing. What follows is a brief introduction to the fundamental note-taking methods that complement our learning and summarizing.

Note-Taking Methods

Outlining

The outlining method of note-taking is the most popular and common form used by high school and college students. It is effective in organizing information in a logical and structured manner. Students frequently and subconsciously revert to outlining when taking notes during a lecture or reading from a textbook. Professionals resort to outlining during meetings and seminars. We can identify the outline method as lists of phrases or statements where the major points appear farthest to the left, followed by their supporting points in succeeding and indented lines.

. . .

Mind Mapping

Mind mapping is a pictorial representation of the main idea and its hierarchy of supporting concepts. It involves writing down a central theme and then thinking of related or secondary themes that radiate around the central theme. The related themes are further deconstructed into ideas or concepts that likewise radiate from them, and so forth. The result is a concept map that graphically depicts the structure of the main idea or theme in terms of its parts. Its appearance also earned it the term "spider diagram.".

Charting

This note-taking method is straightforward and uncomplicated. As the name suggests, it uses charts or arrays to condense and organize notes relative to each other. The method involves splitting a document into columns and rows. The cells created by the intersecting rows and columns are then filled with summaries of information. The result is a table that allows ready access and comparison of data that fall into similar categories.

Sentence

As the name implies, this method's notes create whole statements embodying complete ideas. Unlike simple paragraph writing, this method uses line spacing to separate and distinguish between concepts and ideas.

Introducing a new idea involves writing a new sentence on a separate line. The resulting notes appear as large quantities of sentences arranged in vertical order. Students unaware of more efficient methods of taking notes will inadvertently adopt some version of the sentence method since it does not require any planning or preparation.

The Cornell Method

Many experienced note-takers describe the Cornell Note-taking method as the best technique because of its efficiency and ease of execution. The method's strength lies in its page layout, which consists of two columns, a 7-inch-wide column on the left and the rest of the page on the right. The large right column is the note-taking column, and the 7-inch narrower column at the left is the Cue/Questions/Keyword column. The method comprises five steps respectively entered in the appropriate column – Record, Question, Recite, Reflect, and Review. Finally, the notes are summarized on the next page.

From these brief descriptions, there appears to be little distinction between the methods. They all involve identifying main concepts and ideas supported by secondary ideas or thoughts. However, we typically find that one or some methods better serve our note-taking needs depending on the type of information gathered, which in turn is related to the learning style we resort to when we learn.

Actions Steps

We discussed learning styles as if they were hard-and-fast science. In truth, the validity of learning styles is still being scientifically debated, although their categorization is useful in some situations. [16] Our brain is so complex that we may even combine learning styles and competently apply them, depending upon the type of knowledge being absorbed. The diagram below [17] shows that people may be adept at more than one learning style.

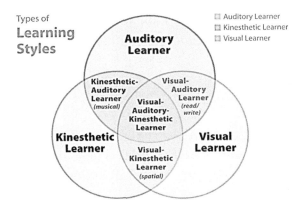

You have been introduced to five note-taking methods: outlining, mind mapping, charting, sentence, and the Cornell method. We haven't delved too deeply into any of these methods yet, but from their brief descriptions, you probably have an idea about which note-taking method or methods different learners prefer. There are seven types of learners in the diagram. Could you match which note-taking method appeals most to each of the groups? Is there a match between the Kolb learning styles and the note-taking methods? Do you think the difference among the learners will matter in their choice of method?

Moving On

Teresa is a gifted student, but the school's teaching style did not align with her preferred learning method. We all should know the style that best complements how our minds absorb and retain information. Our learning style provides a hint about the note-taking method that suits us best. We will take a close look at each of the note-taking methods in the chapters to follow.

Key Takeaways

- There are four core learning styles, according to Neil Fleming's VARK model. These are Visual or spatial, Auditory or aural, Reading and writing or verbal, and Kinesthetic or physical. Each style matches the learning method that individuals prefer and to which they are best accustomed.
- Aside from the VARK, researchers have identified other modes of learning. These are the logical or mathematical, social or interpersonal, and the solitary or intrapersonal learning methods. These expand and complement

Fleming's original core learning styles and address other learning preferences not adequately covered by the first four.

- David Kolb's Learning Style Model is an alternative to the Fleming VARK and expanded model. Under Kolb's model, learning undergoes four stages: concrete experience (feeling), reflective observation (watching), abstract conceptualization (thinking), and active experimentation (doing). Combining the stages leads to Kolb's four learning styles: accommodating, diverging, assimilating, and converging,

- Before taking notes, it is important to understand how to create a written summary of a text or selection. First, read the text with understanding. Second, break the text down into sections. Third, identify the key points in each section. Fourth, write down the key points and explain them. Finally, check the summary against the original text. The summary provides the content of the notes.

- The various learning styles lead to the following note-taking methods: outlining, mind mapping, charting, sentence, and the Cornell method. We shall focus on them in the succeeding chapters.

3

OUTLINING – POINTS AND HIERARCHY

Dinosaur skeletons [1]

C hildren have always held a fascination for dinosaurs. That, of course, includes you and me. I bet you could name each of the dinosaurs above just from the outline of their skeletons. How about giving it a try before you glance at the answers in the footnotes? [2] Remarkably, these animals died off millions of years ago. Yet we know that the T-rex is a carnivore, and while the Triceratops and the Stegosaurus were herbivores, they each defended themselves differently. We have built a world of knowledge around animals long extinct by studying the skeletons they left behind.

When we see the structure of a thing, we get a pretty good idea of what that thing is in its entirety and how it differs from others of its kind, much like dinosaur skeletons. The same is true of abstract ideas put into words. We could read many sentences, paragraphs, and chapters that describe a great deal about an idea, but we don't need all those words to retain the essence of that idea. We could, in many cases, recall much of the original information from a skeleton of that text. That "skeleton" is its outline.

Definition Of Outlining

In the preceding chapter, we described outlining as the most popular method students use because it organizes information in a structured manner. A well-constructed outline contains the important points of a mass of information (such as a text selection, lecture, or chapters in a book) and depicts them according to how they are hierarchically related to each other. Outlining notes is a logical exercise, and it reflects the way we think. We used outlines in note-taking instinctively, even without knowing they had a name. [3]

Examples Of An Outline

The outline is easily identifiable because it uses indentations to visually distinguish between main ideas and supporting ideas. A system of numbers and letters preceding the indented notes can further emphasize the hierarchy of the written points. Headings and subheadings are also helpful in enhancing the structure.

As we progress along with these chapters, you will notice that they are similarly organized. Chapters 3 to 8 follow this general outline:

A. Definition

　1. Example 1
　2. Example 2

B. Advantages of the method

　1. Advantage 1
　2. Advantage 2
　3. Advantage 3

C. Disadvantages of the method

　1. Disadvantage 1
　2. Disadvantage 2
　3. Disadvantage 3

D. Situations when the method is best used

The important points regarding each note-taking method are laid out in the same order to make it easier for us, the readers, to find the specific information we need. The outline categorizes the items of information according to their relationship with one another. In this respect, the outline method of note-taking is quite convenient to use.

But could outlining apply for purposes other than categorizing data?

Certainly. Recall how writing a book report in outline form was part of most reading assignments in elementary and high school. For this purpose, aside from organizing points into categories, we also write down the progression of events, as in relaying the plot or storyline.

Book Report Outline

A. Title: Goldilocks and the Three Bears

B. Author: Robert Southey

C. Characters

- Papa, Mama, and Baby Bear
- Goldilocks

D. Setting

- The forest
- The cottage of the Bear family

E. Plot

- The Bear family went out for a walk in the forest.
- Goldilocks arrived at the Bears' cottage.
- Goldilocks felt hungry. She tasted their porridge and found that:

1. Papa Bear's porridge was too hot.
2. Mama Bear's porridge was too cold.
3. Baby Bear's porridge was just right so she ate it all up

- She tried sitting on their chairs. She found that:

1. Papa Bear's chair was too big.
2. Mama Bear's chair was too hard.
3. Baby Bear's chair was just right but it broke into pieces.

- Goldilocks felt sleepy and went to the bedroom.

1. Papa Bear's bed was too hard.
2. Mama Bear's bed was too soft.
3. Baby Bear's bed was just right.

- Goldilocks fell asleep on Baby Bear's bed.

- The Bears returned from their walk and noticed that:

1. Somebody tasted their porridge and ate up Baby Bear's porridge.
2. Somebody sat on their chairs and broke up Baby Bear's chair.
3. Somebody slept on their beds and was still asleep in Baby Bear's bed.

- The Bears saw Goldilocks, who happened to wake up.
- Goldilocks ran away in fright.

F. Main Takeaway

- Never wander off into the forest by yourself.

There are several irregularities we may observe in the Goldilocks outline. Firstly, many details have been left out, such as how Goldilocks had knocked first several times before entering the house. There is also a short segment in the original story describing how Goldilocks was at home with her mother, who warned her not to wander off. As to form, most noticeable in the outline is that some entries are only words or phrases, while others are complete statements. Some entries are enumerations linked to phrases in colons.

Outlines in informal note-taking need only conform to your comfort and preference. But when outlines are prepared for formal submission, some schools and universities require specific standards to be followed.

Important Pointers To Follow When Outlining

Keep in mind that a good outline for formal submission abides by certain guidelines. [4]

1. Headings must contain information that is already available. For instance, instead of writing "When the war began," you may as well write "Started 1775" when outlining the American revolutionary war. "Reason for the war" should be replaced with "Colonies sought independence from British rule."

2. Minimize unnecessary division. For instance, instead of writing:

1. The incandescent light bulb
2. Inventor: Thomas Edison
3. Date: January 1879
4. Place: Menlo Park, New Jersey

Simply write:

1. The incandescent light bulb
2. Created by Thomas Edison on January 1879 in Menlo Park, New Jersey

3. For an outline intended for submission, the subdivisions should designate "equally important and parallel divisions of the subject as a whole." [5]Here's an example:

Unequal headings	Equal Headings
A. A brief for your home's design	A. A brief for your home's design
a. Budget for materials	a. Budget
b. Find a good location	b. Time frame
c. Choose your lifestyle	c. Room requirements
d. Feng Shui	d. Floor plan

In the left column, the headings are unequal because they involve elements that, while related, pertain to different aspects of the home's design. "Finding a location" might not even be correctly placed in the outline because while the other aspects already relate to the actual design, finding a location is a precedent to it. By comparison, the headings in the right column are equal and relevant aspects that should appear in a home design brief intended for the architect or designer.

4. You may use abbreviations and acronyms for proper nouns or common phrases to speed up note-taking. Remember, though, that sometime in the future, the meanings of shortcuts may be obscured or forgotten. As much as possible, use complete words or phrases followed immediately by the abbreviation in parenthesis, at least when you first refer to the name or phrase. For example:

- National Institute of Allergy and Infectious Diseases (NIAID)
- dead on arrival (DOA)

When you need to refer to them again, using the abbreviation would be fine. That way, you will have a perpetual reminder in the outline itself.

5. Headings of equal rank should not have contents that overlap conceptually. This means that the heading "A" should exclude items in heading "B" and vice versa.

Overlapping	Properly differentiated
A. Indoor dogs	A. Small canine breeds
a. Labrador	a. Yorkshire Terrier
b. Yorkshire Terrier	b. Chihuahua
c. Shih Tzu	c. Miniature Schnauzer
d. Malinois	d. Miniature Pinscher
B. Outdoor dogs	B. Large canine breeds
a. Siberian Husky	a. Black Russian Terrier
b. Doberman	b. Bullmastiff
c. Belgian Shepherd	c. St. Bernard
d. Golden Retriever	d. Giant Schnauzer

The two columns above are lists of dog categories in outline form. In a well-constructed outline, the headings designated "A" and "B" are of equal rank. Therefore, they must not overlap – the items listed under each heading must be mutually exclusive and non-repeating. But the left column shows subdivisions that overlap, while the right column shows subdivisions that are exclusive of each other.

You might say, "In the left column, there are no repetitions, so how could there be overlapping?" The overlap is conceptual. Indoor dogs and outdoor dogs are supposed to be mutually exclusive. But we all know that those dogs listed as "Indoor" also go outdoors for walks, and the dogs categorized as "Outdoor" are also taken indoors by many owners. There is also an actual overlap in the form of a double entry. Among the breeds mentioned, a Malinois is a type of Belgian Shepherd. So, if Belgian Shepherds are outdoor dogs, then Malinoises are outdoor dogs. The outline at the left is, therefore, not proper.

By comparison, the outline at the right has headings designating "Small" and "Large" canine breeds. These are mutually exclusive. You might say, however, "Look, there are Schnauzers and Terriers under both headings. They overlap!" They do not. The Yorkshire and Black Russian Terriers are different breeds, and so are the Miniature and Giant Schnauzers (as their names suggest).

Yorkshire Terrier [6] and Black Russian Terrier [7]

Advantages Of Outlining

1. Outlining makes reviewing the notes easier. Outlines leave out unnecessary details and go direct to the point. You won't have to search over so many words to arrive at the gist of the idea.

2. Outlining shows not only the concepts that make up the content but their relationships with each other as well. The system of indentation and use of numbers and letters (if any) makes understanding the hierarchy of ideas easier. The visual breaks signal to our mind that either a new topic with the same importance or a supporting topic is introduced.

3. By following a structured framework, this method allows us to focus on our lecture or the source presentation without being distracted regarding whether we are getting our notes right.

4. Outlining is flexible and allows for use or combination with other methods or enhancements. If we write an outline in longhand, we can even draw arrows and lines to connect different subtopics and jot down comments on the side. [8]

Aside from its structure, there are no stringent conditions for outlining as a note-taking method. Recall how statements and phrases were both used in the Goldilocks outline. There is no requirement that only statements, or only phrases for that matter, should be used. We can use what devices are available to best capture the idea.

Sometimes we can devise a mental shortcut with arrows or enhance entries with mathematical symbols such as the plus (+) or equal (=) sign, like a pseudo-math equation. For instance, the following lines would be appropriate entries in outlined notes.

- For the native population, colonization = death.
- A harmful deed + criminal intent ⟶ a crime

Note that in these examples, the use of mathematical symbols does not constitute a mathematical expression. Mathematical expressions or solutions may be ill-suited to note-taking via outlining, as we shall see in the next section. But the symbols are used here as shortcuts to denote the equivalence or combination of two or more things.

Disadvantages Of Outlining

1. Outlining requires more thought to organize the ideas meaningfully. This may be difficult to do if the lecture goes too fast or the information is in the form of a video presentation.

2. When the flow of information we receive does not properly sequence the ideas according to their logical relationships, then outlining might not produce the best results.

3. When the lesson involves a lot of mathematical equations and graphs, outlining may not be the appropriate note-taking method because, in this situation, the hierarchical structure breaks down and the indentation system loses its significance.

4. Sometimes, taking down notes in outline form may lead us to leave out important details inadvertently. This happens when we become too intent on paring down the

notes to their most condensed form, so we have less to memorize. When we look at dinosaur skeletons, we have no idea about their skin, color, or soft tissues such as their eyes. So, too, does outlining leave out the information we may later discover that we may need.

Situations When Outlining Is Suitable

When we take notes, more often than not, we defer to the outline method. It's as if, instinctively, we tend to interpret the lessons we hear or the texts we read according to the hierarchical method implicit in outlining. That is far from surprising. The speakers and authors of the texts we study frequently present their material arranged according to a logical order. The main theme may be introduced in the initial statement, followed by supporting points. In reverse order, supporting information may be presented first, leading to the concluding statement that contains the main theme. Either way, a logical order governs the selection, and we jot down notes based on this perceived order. In this scenario, we replicate the thought process of the lecturer or lesson according to the presentation.

Outlining is not ideal for all situations. When the material is not presented following the conventional hierarchical order, we need a more flexible way to capture ideas. For instance, in a brainstorming session, ideas fly about in random order as quickly as they are generated by different people – or even by oneself, in some cases. Ideas randomly presented frequently do not follow a logical pattern, and so it is inconceivable that they could be written out as an outline with main and secondary topics following each other.

Sharon Watson is the author of a blog article [9]where she provides some handy suggestions for teaching students how to create outlines. She observed that most students have difficulty writing outlines because they do not want to take the time or trouble organizing their thoughts. To cross this hurdle, she suggested making outlines out of familiar rather than difficult material. Here are two suggestions.

Grocery Store Outline

Grocery stores have so many items that may be grouped into classes, and each class is broken down further into subgroups and sub-subgroups, etc. When we enter a grocery store, the items are already arranged in such an orderly manner to help customers find the exact item they need. This arrangement can help create an outline easily.

Obtain a free worksheet on which you will write your outline. A worksheet is typically divided into columns that you can use to guide the indentations of your outline. You can choose the notation for the levels, such as I, A, 1, a, and so forth. From the items in the grocery store, list the goods according to categories and groups. You can let the aisle signs and shelf labels guide you.

· · ·

Restaurant Outline

Expanding the exercise, you can classify the types of restaurants in your area or those you became familiar with on your travels, from television shows, the internet, and so forth. You can start with "fine dining," "fast foods," and "bistros," before proceeding to their cultural specialties such as Mexican, Italian, Japanese, or others. Or maybe, you can reverse the level and go with the cultural specialty before the type of service. Under each restaurant classification, write down the restaurant names that fall under them. You can go further and list the restaurant locations below these. Your method of arranging the entries will be your own. As with the grocery store example, you may use a prepared worksheet for this.

These two examples are suggested for those who have not developed the skill for outlining, particularly kids. But the ease of the material will also benefit older individuals who want to build a greater facility for organizing their thoughts into outlines. You can think of more complex topics that you are personally familiar with or select material that you are currently struggling with, as the subject to outline. You can ask the help of a colleague or friend to gain better insight into organizing your thoughts. Comparing your work with that of other individuals or groups is also a good idea. Refine your work until you are satisfied with the results.

Moving On

It is remarkable how our paleontologists have been able to deduce much about dinosaurs based on their skeletons, without seeing their complete anatomies. This is how we can retain much about our lessons by creating good outlines that embody only the important points. The outline, with its indentations and hierarchy of ideas, is the "skeleton" that helps us remember the lesson's vital points. The next chapter will introduce us to another useful note-taking method that will enhance our learning ability.

Key Takeaways

- Outlining is the most popular method of note-taking taught by schools and used by students. It consists of writing down important notes arranged according to the hierarchy of relationships.
- Outlining uses indentations to visually distinguish between main ideas and their supporting concepts. The hierarchy is indicated as well by a system of numbers and letters, bullets and symbols, or headings and subheadings.
- Outlining as a personal note-taking method is flexible and may be adjusted to your preference. When outlines are required for formal

submissions, the school typically specifies pointers students are required to follow.

- Outlining has its advantages. It goes direct to the point and therefore makes reviews easier. Its indentations highlight the hierarchy of ideas. For personal note-taking, outlining is flexible and allows for mental shortcuts.

- Outlining has its disadvantages. It may take longer for the note-taker to organize her thoughts, if the lecture goes too fast or the sequence of ideas is not properly arranged. Some types of information are not appropriate for outlining and may be unintentionally left out.

4

MIND MAPPING - CREATING ROADS TO KNOWLEDGE

Before the covid pandemic lockdown, my husband and I were fortunate to visit our grown-up children, who now live in Vancouver, and to spend Christmas 2019 with them. My daughter had just started work at a wonderful school called Mount Pleasant, a short distance from where they lived. One evening, after an administrative meeting, Nikki called and asked us to pick her up at work as it had grown cold and quite dark outside. "How do we get there by car from the house?" her Dad asked. Our residence was located on Kerr Street.

Our daughter replied: "Go down Kerr and onto Rupert Street until you reach Kingsway. At Kingsway, turn left and go straight. You will pass Victoria Drive, but don't turn; just go straight. You'll also pass Kensington Cedar Cottage, then after that Fraser Street, but don't turn, just keep going straight. When you reach East Broadway, turn right. You will come to a roundabout but just continue straight to stay on Brunswick Street. Then turn right onto East 7th Avenue, and presto! You're here!"

"Nikki, were you reading from Google Maps?" I asked. It occurred to me that she mentioned several unimportant places since we still just had to keep going straight. "Okay, so I thought you'd like a few landmarks to confirm that you're on track," she said. I looked up Google Maps and found this.

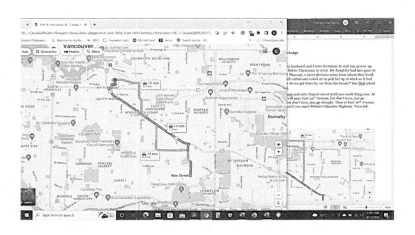

Directions from Kerr Street to Mount Pleasant Elementary, Vancouver, British Columbia [1]

"Hmmmph," I thought, discarding the piece of paper I was frantically jotting notes on. My husband took one look at the map and said, "Got it." Just to be sure, I took a screenshot of the Google Map display, and off we went. We were back home with Nikki in half an hour, just before the flurry turned into a squall.

Defining The Mind Map

A roadmap is used to visually chart the route from a source to a destination. In much the same way, a mind map draws the connections that link ideas with each other. It is "a visual tool which can be used in determining the preliminary information, thoughts, comprehensions, cognitive structures, and conceptual relations of students and in the improvement of conceptual understanding." [2] With our first introduction to mind mapping, we immediately appreciate the ease of using maps compared to following verbal directions. It brings to mind the old saying, "A picture is worth a thousand words," and its corollary, "A picture is easier to remember than a thousand words."

Mind mapping is a strong graphical technique that aims to utilize the brain's full capacity.[3] It was developed as a method for effectively generating ideas by association. Mind mapping encourages active learning [4] and associating present information with new information. [5]

The mind mapping technique involves writing down a central theme and thinking of new and related themes that are written down as radiating from the center. [6]You could think of it as an organized method of brainstorming [7]since you begin with the main idea and then allow your mind to wander and explore concepts that are interconnected with this main topic.

Mind maps have four important features: [8]

A word or image at the center of the map provides the focus on the subject.

- Branches emanating from the center develop the main themes of the focal point.
- The connected lines of the branches each lead to a keyword or idea.
- The branches indicate the thought structure, such that the more remote a word or idea is from the center, its association narrows to the main idea.

How To Create A Mind Map

The University of Adelaide [9]suggests the following five steps to create a mind map.

1. Place the central theme or main concept at the center of the page. You may find it easier to situate your page in landscape orientation as it helps for drawing purposes.

2. Use lines, arrows, speech bubbles, branches, and different colors (if you so choose) to show the connection between the main theme and the other ideas that stem from it. The bubbles contain the ideas, but do not forget to draw the lines or arrows as they define the relationships.

3. Do not create an artistic masterpiece with a lot of embellishments. You should draw your elements quickly and simply without major pauses or editing. Keep in mind that, in most probability, your initial impulses are

correct as you situate the idea in the branch or direction that makes the most sense to you. In the early stage of mind mapping, it is best to consider every possibility, even those you may not eventually use.

4. If you choose to color your work, let each color symbolize something different. They could represent how you regard the idea. For instance, use blue for essential ideas you feel you must include in your final essay, green for ideas you think are promising but not sure of, and orange for ideas you need to check out with your teacher. The selection of colors and what they mean is entirely your choice, but you must remain consistent throughout the final stage of the mind-mapping process.

5. Leave some space on the page. Your mind map may be a work in progress, and over a period of time, you may want to develop it further by adding new ideas and details as you develop your thoughts on the topic. You can consider using an A4 or A3-sized paper.

Example Of A Mind Map

Let's see if we can understand the ideas it conveys, given a mind map. The central concept of the mind map below is "Strategies for Taking Action," but unless we read the title "Strategies for Climate Change," then we would not know the goal "Taking Action" refers to.

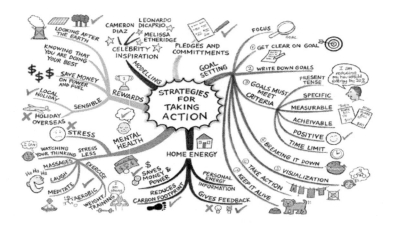

Mind Mapping "Strategies for Climate Change" Topic [10]

Various branches stem from the main idea: Home Energy, Mental Health, Rewards, Modelling, Pledges and Commitments, and Goal Setting. Are the ideas categorically alike? Not even close. "Mental health" has nothing in common with Pledges and Commitments, nor do these concepts share similarities with Home Energy and so on. But each topic can be conceptually linked to strategies for addressing climate change.

Even adjacent branches along the same topic may be categorically different. "Write down goals" is an action, while "Goals must meet criteria" identifies a set of requirements. There is no hard and fast rule for the ideas on a mind map, except that it makes sense to the note-taker. Based on our reading of the mind map above, we can identify some advantages and disadvantages we might encounter when using this technique.

Advantages Of Mind Mapping

1. Mind maps differ significantly from the traditional note-taking methods such as outlining, but their use of graphics improves students' visual recall of information prone to be rendered this way.

2. Mind mapping is a suitable method for taking notes at a meeting or lecture. It is the ideal technique for those who have the habit of doodling when taking notes during a talk. You would also be able to keep track of the lecturer should they skip from one topic to another because a mind map does not follow a logical sequence. You can skip branches in random order.

3. For the same reason as No.2 above, mind mapping is an excellent way of visualizing complex tasks. Trying to envision a complex task in serial order can be difficult. You forget details in-between that you would have to squeeze in if you were doing an outline or paragraph. With a mind map, you can also break down a large undertaking into smaller parts and focus on these smaller tasks individually.

4. It is a great method to partner with to-do lists. "To-do" lists enumerate the tasks you intend, well, to do. But in a regular to-do list, since the tasks are written down one after the other, it might give you the mindset that you should also perform them one after the other when such was not your intention. A mind map that supplements a to-do list does not impose any serial order on the tasks, so you are free to think about them randomly if you so wish.

5. It is an effective way to mix multiple type lists. As in brainstorming, ideas of different types pop up in your head related to the main theme. You can start with different lists on a mind map by creating other branches: one that lists tasks, another listing people's names, another that lists color schemes, and so on.

There is one unique advantage of mind mapping over the other methods of note-taking. Students who regard English as a second language, particularly those in higher academic programs, will find mind mapping extremely useful. Mind mapping foregoes strict adherence to grammatical structure, syntactical accuracy, and correct spelling. Foreign students enrolled in English-speaking universities are typically required to meet the standards of academic writing, which is more demanding than merely conversational English. Students find themselves struggling not only with language differences such as vocabulary and grammar, but also with psychosocial considerations (e.g., a sense of class community) self-efficacy, and writing anxiety. [11]

Writing academic-standard English is a different skill from understanding spoken English, as in a lecture or other oral presentations. When we are conversant with a foreign language, we frequently get the gist of conversations and imbibe the concepts they relay. We can confirm our understanding through the speaker's body language and facial expression. We can easily note down, in simple words, arrows, and drawings, the information we learned. But we are at a loss if we are to write down complete sentences, or even phrases, stating what we learned. Even if we were able to, we would need to devote more time and attention to thinking about what to write, that we would be distracted from the lecture or presentation.

The mind map presents an opportunity to shortcut the note-taking process by rendering the ideas and their relationships in graphic form, much like in doodling. You can translate your thoughts into a picture that has meaning for you.

Disadvantages Of Mind Mapping

1. Mind mapping is laborious. The effort a person exerts while mind mapping depends on his disposition. Doodlers may find mind mapping a walk in the park. But for others not inclined to draw, it takes too much work.

2. Mind mapping is time-consuming. Typically, those who find that this technique takes too much work will also find that it takes too much of their time.

3. Some may feel that they lose information when they try to condense it into a mind map. It is difficult to elaborate on details in mind mapping. Therefore, this technique might not be ideal for complicated topics we think of as "rocket science."

4. It is easy to over-complicate a mind map as you add to it. Furthermore, if you are not using digital mind mapping software, the result can be messy on paper.

5. Analyzing a mind map completed after many stages can be confusing. You could have revisited the diagram multiple times and added to it over several weeks so that when you have finally concluded your mind map, there are areas that are difficult to relate to in the same context.

Let's Try It

Consider the following selection:

A mind map allows a user to record a great deal of information in the form of linked ideas with keywords and images. Essentially, a user records or inscribes gathered information on a page while showing the relationships between the concepts involved. According to Zhang et al (2010)." It fully utilizes both the left and right brain, and can be used as a memory aided tool in any field of study, work and life. The use of mind mapping can be assisted with "the adoption of colors, images, codes, and multidimensional approaches to help human memory, so that one could concentrate the mind on the central part, which is, the crucial subject." If students can represent or manipulate a complex set of relationships in a diagram, they are more likely to understand those relationships, remember them, and be able to analyze their component parts. This, in turn, promotes "deep" and not "surface" approaches to learning (Biggs 1987; Entwistle 1981; Marton and Saljo 1976a, b; Ramsden 1992). Secondly, for most people, maps are also much easier to follow than verbal or written descriptions, although reservations need to be made in terms of the kinds of "maps" under consideration, for not all maps are equal (Larkin and Simon 1987; Mayer and Gallini 1990). Thirdly, the work involved in mapmaking requires more active engagement on the part of the learner, and this too leads to greater learning (Twardy 2004). "Using Mind Mapping as a study technique": Farrand et al. (2002) shows, retention and recall are better among students when mind maps were used as a study technique. However, they point out that the users must be motivated towards the use of mind maps, i.e. the students must enjoy using it and obviously be conversant in their use. Chan (2004) studied whether mind mapping can be used as a pre-writing strategy to help explore and generate ideas for writing.

The text above is an excerpt from a paragraph in a scholarly article that examined the facility of mind mapping as a note-taking technique for university-level students. [12] I chose a short article from which I expected to create a simple mind map, just to illustrate the technique. As I was reading the text, I started to draw my mind map based on my key takeaways from the selection. What do you observe as you compare the text from the paragraph above and the mind map I created from it?

A mind map of the text from the scholarly article [13]

1. The mind map is easier to understand than the selection. The complicated words and statements are reduced to their main points. It is also easier to remember.

2. Important points and related ideas and their related ideas are structured in the mind map. The branches do not have to be logically and categorically related to each other, as long as they are logically related to the node to which they are connected.

3. Much of the details present in the selection are left out in the mind map. For instance, all the citations that appear in the paragraph are gone, and the explanations of the points raised are reduced to mere phrases. It is up to your mind to fill them in when re-reading the mind map.

4. The same mind map that is useful for the note-taker may not hold the same usefulness or efficacy for other people. The mind map reflects your frame of mind. Just as with any method that does not fully explain a thought or idea, a mind map will be meaningful to the one who created it to a degree that others may not understand or appreciate.

So, if we were to use the above mind map to compose a literature review, it would be inadequate because it left out all necessary citations. However, the map is quite adequate as a tool to recall answers for a test.

Action Steps

Let's have some fun doing this activity. You may do this manually, or use mind-mapping software if you are familiar with one. The following are a few suggested topics that I think will have many aspects people will immediately call to mind.

- Coronavirus pandemic 2019-2022
- Planning a wedding
- Senior year in high school or college
- Preparing for the birth of your first baby
- Going on your first pleasure trip to a foreign country

Choose one of the topics above, or if you have one better in mind, start with that. The topic you choose must be something that has relevance to you, presents you with a lot of possibilities, and is relatively complex to organize your thoughts around. Opt out of the obvious shortcuts – for instance, don't say "Hire a wedding planner" to plan your wedding. Think of everything you need to do by yourself, such as choosing the venue, making the guest list, selecting the menu for the reception, and so forth. The idea is to create a mind map as detailed and expanded as possible.

Write the main topic at the center of your paper, and encase it in its bubble. Then begin writing the next level of related topics around this center, encasing each in its bubble. Draw lines or arrows, whichever you prefer, linking the second-level topics to the main topic. Repeat the process for each second-level topic, creating a third level about them. Make sure that each new topic has a logical link to the higher-level topic to which it is connected. Each successive level will contain increasingly narrower topics than the one that preceded it.

Work in this manner, including fresh ideas that pop into your head – after all, you are undertaking a brainstorming process. When you feel you have exhausted everything worthy to be included, take a look at your mind map in its entirety. Are there redundant items? Are there any important items missed? See how you could further refine it until you are satisfied. You may color-code your bubbles or illustrate some items if you feel it is significant for your purpose.

Now imagine revisiting this mind map in five years, maybe ten. What do you think it would reveal to you about your current state of mind? Do you think your ideas would be as relevant then as they were when you created the mind map?

Moving On

Finding our way to our desired destination can be very much facilitated by a map. For those of us gifted with sight, a single picture conveys the totality of a concept that would otherwise take many words to convey. That is also the advantage of mind mapping. Note-takers forego the use of verbal communication when they have the benefit of a mind map. In the following chapter, we discuss another note-taking method that uses a spatial or visual arrangement of related texts to aid learning and retention.

Key Takeaways

- Mind mapping is a note-taking method designed to record and structure related ideas graphically or pictorially. It is also a method aimed at generating ideas by association in the same way brainstorming does.
- To create a mind map, locate the main theme at the center of the paper. Using lines, arrows, speech bubbles, branches, and other visual tools, connect the secondary ideas to the main theme. Similarly, link new ideas to the secondary ones, and branch out further as needed.
- A great advantage - it does not rely on any particular language, so weaknesses in grammar and semantics are circumvented. It is an excellent way to visualize complex tasks, and is effective in mixing multiple-type lists.
- Potential disadvantages - it can be laborious and time-consuming if you are not inclined to draw. It can also be confusing if you have difficulty organizing complex ideas and condensing them into a diagram. The results can be messy and, in the end, analyzing a mind map after undergoing many stages could be confounding.

5

SENTENCES – EXPLAINING WHOLE IDEAS

Like most teachers, I seldom give tests requiring essay answers. We would rather give tests that require objective answers, like true or false, multiple choice, or fill-in-the-blank items. There's a simple reason for this – objective answers are easier to correct and grade. Questions requiring essay answers are more difficult to evaluate because they necessitate a subjective assessment. Teachers expect no two essay questions to be the same. They must, therefore, read and evaluate the merits of each answer to assign a proper score.

One time, contrary to my usual style, I decided to give an essay exam. I did not have the time to prepare an objective item test. So, I wrote just one question on the board: "Why is a long-term strategy better when investing in stocks?"

Oh, there are so many possible answers. For one, long-term investing is less risky. Another one is its corollary proposition, that short-term investing is much riskier. Still, another is that playing the market or day trading, a form of short-term "investing," is much like gambling. I would have given any of these answers, including several others, full credit because they are the layman's expression of the same idea. Besides, I was a generous teacher.

One paper piqued my interest. "Long-term stock investing gives investors the benefit of the full fundamental value and growth of their companies." Hey, that's a pretty good answer. Student A was paying attention. Then I came across another paper. "A long-term stock investor will benefit from the full fundamental value and growth of the stock he buys." Hmmm. Almost the same words. Is something going on? It was not long before I saw Student C's answer: "Long-term stock investors tend to gain the benefit of the full fundamental value and growth of the companies whose stocks they buy." Uh-oh. I came across Students D and E, two more answers similarly worded. What should I think?

I summoned the five "suspects" to a private conference. I opened with a stern challenge. "Okay, whoever confesses to cheating in an exam will just have to complete a repeat exam. Those who don't confess will be sent to the Dean of Student Affairs for disciplinary action."

The five students stared at me with wide-eyed innocence and disbelief at my accusation. "We did not cheat!" they seemed to protest in silence. Then Student A said, "Why do you think we cheated, Professor?" I showed them their test papers and their mirrored answer. "I believe you copied from each other. How else would you explain this?"

Then one by one, the five students took out their notebooks and showed me their notes. They had taken down my lecture almost word-for-word. It was remarkable because they could have been stenographers in a court of law or secretaries taking down their boss's dictation. It was true that they did not copy from each other during the exam; they didn't even sit close to each other. What happened was that they committed my lecture to writing and then to memory. So, when I asked the lesson's focal question, the students quoted my own lecture.

After they completed a validating activity, I gave them all A's.

Defining The Sentence Method

I do not recommend rote memorization; I told my students that I would prefer it if they understood the lesson and answered the test question in their own words. But I do admire students who try to get the most out of the class lectures or presentations by recording as much information as possible. They do this by mentally articulating what they heard or saw in complete statements, then writing them down. This is known as the sentence method of note-taking.

The sentence method is one of the most rudimentary or "bare bones" types of note-taking. As the name implies, it involves taking notes by writing down whole sentences. It does not involve fancy formats or representations, nor simultaneous or critical analysis. This method foregoes shortcuts and abbreviations, but simply conveys whole ideas as in conversations.

The difference between the sentence method of note-taking and writing whole paragraphs of notes is that, in the note-taking method, the line spacing separates ideas and concepts from each other. When you encounter a new thought, you write it down as a complete idea on a new line. The result is a group of many sentences arranged in vertical order.

The sentence method is a collection of ideas arranged in no particular order. New ideas are written down as fresh sentences, each on a new line, without an attempt to organize them. This is where the method differs from paragraph writing. Paragraphs are structured such that the first sentence is a topic sentence, the next three or four sentences are supporting statements, and the final sentence is a concluding statement.

How To Take Notes Using Sentences

1. Write down each sentence on a separate line. Try to capture the full thought of what the lecturer says. It is not necessary to write down the exact words but preserve the most important ideas in the manner they were presented

or stated. As far as possible, write the important words used by the professor. Be prepared to write very fast.

2. Number the sentences you wrote down in the first step. This helps you make better sense of the notes and provides you with a tool to organize them.

3. Review your notes according to how you wrote them down and numbered them. Rewriting is not needed, but check for any misspelled or typographical errors. There are a couple of tips to make the review process easier.

a.As you write down your sentences, distinguish wherever possible among the different, unrelated topics by creating a line break between them. This helps make the review process easier afterward.

b.While rewriting your notes after the lecture, consider combining this method with another note-taking method. It might take up more of your time, but you will greatly improve your final notes.

When To Best Use The Sentence Method

The sentence method is especially useful under certain circumstances, such as:

- When the lecture goes fast and you have not prepared for it;
- When the lessons do not follow a particular sequence or structure;
- If the information does not require reviewing;

- When you did not prepare for your usual note-taking method before the lecture; or
- When you have to deal with a complex note-taking session divided into longer batches of information such as lectures, podcasts, or presentations.

An apt generalization for when the sentence method is best used is when no other method is available or appropriate. The "bare-bones" writing sentences method is also a catch-all method, allowing for various odds and ends. The fifth situation – when the note-taking session is complex – is best addressed with the sentence method since no one method might suit the situation.

So, what would sentence notes look like? Here's an excellent example provided by Sander Tamm [1]:

Date: March 23, 2021   Topic: Sleep disorders

1. Sleep terrors occur at stage 4 of NREM
2. Nightmares have no consistent duration
3. Sleepwalkers cannot recall their sleepwalking
4. There is no known cure for nightmares
5. A common cause of sleepwalking is fatigue
6. Sleepwalkers are easily awakened
7. Sleepwalking occurs during NREM sleep
8. Sleep terrors: no recollection of content
9. Sleep terrors occur within 15-90 min of sleep
10. Sleep terrors last up to 20 min per episode
11. There are 80+ types of sleep disorders
12. Most common sleep disorder is insomnia
13. Sleep apnea is another common sleep disorder
14. Sleepwalkers have higher CAP cycles and rate
15. CAP means Cyclic Alternating Pattern
16. 1 to 5 % of adults experience parasomnias
17. Sleep groaning is catathrenia
18. Parasomnias often include strange movement
19. Increasing REM sleep is highly beneficial
20. Insomnia is often co-morbid
21. Types: acute, transient, and chronic insomnia

The first impression we get is that the notes appear monolithic, like "a large single vertical block of stone." [2]The lack of spatial relationship between notes contributed to this impression. It also makes structuring the notes difficult and time-consuming. This is why this method is recommended when a thorough review or reorganization of the notes is not necessary.

However, the notes are not entirely without structure. Each idea corresponds to a sentence, and the sentences are numbered. Assigning a number to each statement is the key to referencing the notes. While it may appear wieldy, "the meaning of a statement written down as a sentence – and not just a collection of words – is often clearer and easier to decipher." [3]

Should the notes remain in their original form? There are occasions when the original notes are helpful, such as when they are retained to settle future doubts about the speaker's meaning or specific expressions. When the note-taker is not sure about what the lecturer means, writing down exact words or phrases would support future research.

However, rewriting and reviewing sentence notes is highly recommended. The legibility of notes taken on the fly can decrease sharply in time and with the volume of notes taken. The numbered statements should be rewritten in a new place and in a style that enhances the connections between them. The result will be to consolidate the information and render it in a form that facilitates retention.

Advantages Of The Sentence Method

The sentence method is advantageous because:

1. It is simple and easy to use. Most students who have no training in taking notes automatically revert to sentence note-taking. Expressing ideas in sentence form is the most natural way of capturing the meaning conveyed in a lecture or speech.

2. It requires little preparation or planning to execute. Other note-taking methods require some preparation,

either mental or physical. Mental preparation involves structuring categories or information in your mind. You may need to do some reading ahead of the activity. Physical preparation involves preparing columns, charts, or diagrams into which you will write the information as they are related to each other. In the sentence method, all you need is a blank piece of paper and an open mind.

3. It is versatile and can be used for any subject or lecture. When you are not sure about the topic or specific content of the lecture or speech, it is best to start with a blank slate and a "bare-bones" or generic method. The sentence method could also accommodate mathematical equations and illustrations if such are conveyed in the activity.

4. You don't need to spend time or energy organizing your thoughts or analyzing the ideas to fit any particular order. This, of course, refers to the delivery of the lecture or activity. Organizing and reviewing notes should always be undertaken after the activity to gain the full benefit of the notes taken.

5. The most important advantage of the sentence method is that it gives order to the meaning. The meaning of a full sentence, in contrast to a phrase or a few words, is clearer and easier to contemplate. A full sentence preserves the original meaning of the speaker.

Disadvantages Of The Sentence Method

The sentence method can also be disadvantageous because:

1. It is one of the most inefficient methods of taking notes. Organizing large quantities of sentence notes into more structured notes can be very difficult. Space relationship between notes is lacking or absent in sentence notes. Also, the absence of indentation does not show the links between topics and subtopics.

2. Very quick handwriting or typing may be necessary, particularly when the lecture delivery is fast. When this happens, the main points and important concepts are difficult to separate from minor details due to a lack of time. As a result, reviewing sentence notes can be slow and time-consuming. Sentence notes do not aid in memorization or retention

3. The sentence method is unsuitable when the teaching style or the conduct of classes tends to be chaotic. Since the sentence method follows the flow and sequence of the discussion, if the discussion is not organized and systematic, the resulting sentence notes will be erratic.

4. The greatest disadvantage of the sentence note-taking method is the last step, the review and revision of the material after the session. Of course, you can take sentence notes using an electronic notebook or laptop. Frequently, you will likely be taking notes by hand. As the lecture progresses, the legibility of your notes will tend to

decrease as your hand tires. There may come a point when your handwriting will be difficult even for you to decipher. For this reason, it is important to rewrite and consolidate your notes as soon as possible, so that you may preserve much of the information you gathered from the lecture.

An important drawback of learning from notes gathered using the sentence method is the likelihood that you might be inadvertently suspected of plagiarism. Frequently, sentence notes closely adhere to the original statements from the source. Sentence note-takers seldom paraphrase what they hear. If students review notes that closely mimic other people's words, they may be unintentionally committing plagiarism or open themselves to accusations of such.

Action Steps

Let's practice taking down notes in sentences.

1. First, identify a source of information that is delivered verbally and that is 15 to 30 minutes long. For this activity, you could select a live lecture, an online video lecture, a narrated documentary video, or some other source. You may try a YouTube video on a topic that interests you.

2. After selecting your source, arm yourself with paper and a writing instrument or alternatively, an electronic device with a keyboard such as a laptop, iPad, or notebook.

3. When you are ready, switch on the lecture or narrated documentary. Write down the important statements you hear from the lecture as if you were taking down notes for class. Follow the sentence method: start a new statement on a new line, and number them as you go along.

4. Even though your source is a recording, do not interrupt the lecture/narration while you catch up with your notes.

5. At the end of the lecture/narration, look through the notes you have written down. Evaluate your experience. Are your statements well-written? Is your writing legible to the end? What would you do differently to improve your note-taking using the sentence method?

Keep the notes you wrote down for this exercise. You will need them for a later chapter.

Moving On

The sentence note-taking method has its merits, particularly when you are unprepared for the lecture or unskilled in other methods. But as Students A, B, C, D, and E found out, learning directly from sentence notes the way they took them is deficient. Remembering the words is not the same as learning the lesson. Other note-taking techniques are more effective at building critical thinking skills as the information is received. The next chapter shows us one such method.

Key Takeaways

- The sentence method is one of the most fundamental note-taking techniques. Notes are written down in complete sentences, oftentimes the same sentence given in the lecture. Each sentence is written in a new line and numbered for reference.
- The greatest advantage of the sentence method is its simplicity. You do not need extra training or preparation to take notes in sentences. You are not required to analyze or organize your notes as you take them down.
- This method is best used when the lecture or activity goes fast, when you have not made preparations for the note-taking session, when the activity does not follow a homogeneous format, and when no other note-taking method is appropriate for the type of information conveyed by the lecture or activity.
- Drawbacks to the sentence method include the lack of space relationship between notes, difficulty in reviewing and restructuring the notes post-lecture, the need for speedy handwriting or typing, and the likelihood of illegible handwritten notes during lengthy note-taking activities.

6

CHARTING METHOD – SORTING THINGS OUT

Annie was a young doctor working at a hospital abroad and trying to gain enough experience to set up her own practice in family medicine. After ten years abroad, she came home for a vacation. Her younger sister, Lily, was already married with her first child, Arlyne, just two years old. A few days after Annie's arrival, her little niece came down with a fever and a heavy cold.

Lily, being a first-time mom, was beside herself with worry, and was only too relieved that her sister was around. After a brief examination, Annie prescribed medicine for the baby and gave Lily the following instructions. "I want you to record her vitals. Take her temperature every four hours, and if she has a fever, give her a teaspoon of Calpol. Then three times a day, preferably after meals, give her a teaspoon of Dimetapp, an expectorant, and Loviscol, a mucolytic. Do this for as long as she has her cold symptoms. Then for the next seven days, twice a day, give her the antibiotic, infant dose."

Lily gave her a puzzled stare. "Can we write all this down?" she suggested. Annie took a clean sheet of paper and wrote down the following:

Arlyne	June 1		June 2	June 3

Temperature
- Record reading
  every four
  hours
	6 am
	10 am
	2 pm
	6 pm
	10 pm
		101.5	6 am
			10 am
			2 pm
			6 pm
			10 pm
				6 am
				10 am
				2 pm
				6 pm
				10 pm

Calpol for fever
- 1 tsp. every four
  hours if temp
  reading exceeds
  99.5 deg.
	6 am
	10 am
	2 pm
	6 pm
	10 pm
		√	6 am
			10 am
			2 pm
			6 pm
			10 pm
				6 am
				10 am
				2 pm
				6 pm
				10 pm

Dimetapp - 1 tsp. 3X a day	6 am 12 noon 6 pm	√	6 am 12 noon 6 pm	6 am 12 noon 6 pm
Loviscol - 1 tsp. 3X a day	6 am 12 noon 6 pm	√	6 am 12 noon 6 pm	6 am 12 noon 6 pm
Amoxicillin - 1 tsp. 2X a day, 7 days	6 am 6 pm	√	6 am 6 pm	6 am 6 pm
Urine	√ light yellow			
Stool	√ formed			

Chart 1: Medical Chart

"See, I've filled up the first entries for you, based on what we've already done. I want you to write down her temperature reading every four hours. I've written down the schedule so it will be easy for you to follow. Then going downwards, place a checkmark beside the schedule every time you give her medicines. Also, note down when she goes to the bathroom. Call me if her symptoms persist, or if there are any new developments," Annie said. Then she smiled reassuringly. "Don't worry! She'll be fine!"

Defining The Charting method

This method of note-taking uses charts to condense and organize notes. A chart is a set of vertical and horizontal lines that divide the space on a piece of paper into columns and rows. During note-taking, the spaces in the columns and rows are then filled with summaries of information. This format for note-taking facilitates the efficient comparison between ideas organized according to criteria and records.

The story that opens this chapter demonstrates the use of a chart to document a patient's progress during treatment. The use of charts is a prevalent practice in the medical field, and nurses are trained to follow standard procedures in charting, including:

- Narrative nurses' notes;
- Charting by exception (CBE);
- SOAP(IER) notes (acronym for subjective, objective, assessment, plan, intervention, evaluation, and revision which form the chart contents); and
- PIE (problems, intervention, and evaluations) charts.[1]

We will not go in-depth into these types of charts as they are for a particular specialization. We present it here only to illustrate how charting serves as a highly functional and efficient tool in some well-defined applications. For the medical profession, standard chart formats provide a reliable documentation and communication tool for doctors, nurses, and other medical specialists to acquire and convey vital information about a patient.

It is conceivable that every profession or industry would have its set of standard charts, given their usefulness in recording information considered important in that field. We also create charts for ourselves to record notes about what we consider important for our use. Making charts is simple. Here are the three basic steps to do it.

How To Chart

1. Before taking notes, identify the topics and categories according to which you will classify the information.

2. Create the chart by drawing vertical lines that divide the paper into columns. You may draw vertical lines immediately, or as you proceed from one topic or record to the next. Allow for enough space in each box to contain the written information.

3. If new categories or topics are encountered, draw a new chart. Each manually-drawn chart can accommodate only a two-dimensional array (i.e., a data structure with contiguous elements). The two dimensions comprise the row and column headings respectively. If the data must

reflect three or more dimensions, then create a new chart. One chart may not contain all the information you need, in which case you can construct more charts related to each other.

Of the three steps mentioned, probably the most difficult to execute is the first step. It requires us to have a comprehensive understanding of the information to classify ideas effectively. Take the example on the next page.

Chart 2 is a simple, one-dimensional chart. Its categories are aligned at the top, and the notes classified under each category are arranged as columns. It is a chart useful for understanding aspects of the charting method, and additional entries may be made at the end of each column. Note, however, that notes aligned as rows have no bearing on each other. This is a one-dimensional chart.

Example Of Charting

Monday March 12, 2012
page 1 of 1

How?	Advantages	Disadvantages	When to use it?
Set up your paper in columns and table headings.	Helps pull out the relevant information.	Can be a hard system to learn to use.	If you'll be tested on facts and relationships.
The headings could be categories covered in the lecture.	Reduces the amount of writing required.	You will need to know what content is being covered at the beginning of the lecture.	If content is heavy and presented quickly — such as a history course with dates, people, events, etc.
Insert information (words, phrases, main ideas, etc.) into the appropriate column	Provides easy review for memorizing facts and studying comparisons and relationships		If you want to make an overview of the whole course on one big paper.

Chart 2: Charting method of note-taking [2]

The entries along the rows are not related. Contrast this with the first chart drawn by Annie in the opening anecdote. Entries along the columns are related by the date they were recorded. Entries along the rows are related by the type of information, such as the temperature readings taken at specific schedules and the checklist recording when a particular medicine was administered. This is a two-dimensional chart, with one dimension referring to the categories along the column headings, and a second dimension referring to the categories along the row designations.

Another example of a two-dimensional chart is what may appear in a teacher's record book.

Chart All	Total	Letter Grade	Math Practice 1	Math Review 1	Student Word Probl.	Word Problems Pr...	Word Problem Test	Fractions Practice 1	Fractions Classwork	Fractions Practice...	Fractions Practice 2	Final Fractions	Fractions Questions	Fractions Quiz	Homework	Classwork	Quiz	Test
Date Due			8/22	8/23	8/25	8/26	9/1	9/7	9/9	9/16	9/20	9/23	1/25	1/25				
Category			Home	Clas	Clas	Home	Test	Home	Clas	Quiz	Home	Clas	Home	Quiz				
Possible Pts			10	10	10	15	100	10	10	100	10	20	10	30	10%	50%	15%	25%
Average	**91.16**	**A**	**89.5**	**83**	**89.5**	**93.3**	**91.9**	**90.5**	**93.7**	**92.1**	**85.8**	**93.5**	**85**	**95.3**	**89.29**	**90.68**	**92.81**	**91.9**
Brown, Louise	93.72	A	9	8	9	15	99%	B	10	97%	10	18		28	95.45	90	96.15	99
Carr, Harry	91.14	A	9	8	8	15	98%	B	10	100%	5	17		30	86.36	86	100	98
Cox, Robert	88.97	B	8	9	8	12	97%	A	10	88%	7	16		27	84.55	86	88.46	97
Ford, Frances	94.43	A	9	10	9	12	97%	A		86%	10	20	1/2	26	82.73	97.5	87.69	97
Freeman, Lisa	89.9	A	8	9	8	12	89%	C	10	96%	8	20		28	64.55	94	94.62	89
Hart, Dorothy	89.15	B	9	8	8	13	88%	A	9	95%		19		30	92.22	88	96.15	86
Hernandez, Samuel	91.35	A	10	7	10	14	100%	B	10	83%	10	17		28	95.45	88	85.38	100
Jackson, Tina	92.48	A	9	9	9	15	86%	A	10	89%	8	20		29	93.64	96	90.77	86
Johnson, Bruce	88.2	B	9	8	8	15	100%	A	8	86%	10	17	1/2	30	88.18	82	89.23	100
Montgomery, Willie	91.67	A	8	7	9	15	89%	A	10	96%	7	20		29	90	92	96.15	89
Moore, Juan	92.9	A	9	9	10	14	98%	C	10	86%	10	19		27	73.64	96	86.92	98
Oliver, Julie	94.28	A	10	10	10	15	96%	A	7	89%	8	20		30	95.45	94	91.54	96
Olson, Harry	88.13	B	9	8	8	14	86%	B	10	85%	10	18		30	93.64	88	88.46	88
Peterson, Robin	94.21	A	8	9	10	13	98%	A	8	95%	7	20		27	89.36	94	93.85	98

Chart 3: Teacher's record book [3]

All of us who have taught in school are familiar with this type of chart where we record students' performance in class. The rows are assigned to students' names, while the columns are assigned to the criteria for judging their performance. You could have attendance, tests or exams, class participation, homework, and whatever activity students are graded on. The cells at the intersection of the rows and columns contain the specific grade the student (recorded in the row label) earned for the activity (indicated in the column heading). The students' names and the activities comprise the two dimensions.

If a third category is needed, then another chart is needed. Say, if the teacher handles five classes, the class comprises the third category. A class designation may be a different course or subject for the same set of students (i.e., the same section), or it may be the same course or subject but a different section. The latter is usually the case since teachers or professors typically specialize in one course or subject. In this case, the teacher creates a new chart for the new subject or section if she were using manual charts.

It is possible to have a single chart for more than two dimensions if you are adept at using electronic charting. An application software known as Excel allows us to create charts or tables with three or more dimensions.[4]Having a single data table that holds multiple dimensions is very useful because it is easier to calculate numerical data or sort and count alphanumeric data according to a combination of the different dimensions.

Advantages Of Charting

Based on our cursory discussion of charting, we can already appreciate several of its advantages. The charting method helps you achieve the following:

1. Charting reduces the amount of writing necessary and is useful for capturing high-yield information. Just imagine the size of the cells or boxes into which you have to compress the notes. Charting successfully requires that you condense the notes to their most concise form. This is a skill you will need to master if you use charting as your main note-taking method.

2. Charting will make you proficient at quickly organizing notes as you write them down. As you listen to the information, your mind is already deep in the process of analyzing it and assigning it to the proper box in the chart. You also learn to filter out any extraneous information, leaving only the important details to write down.

3. Charts are useful for comparing similar topics. In a chart, related data points are juxtaposed with each other. This arrangement makes the notes naturally conducive for comparison. A bird's eye view of the chart immediately gives you a sense of the contiguous notes' similarities and differences.

4. Charts help students to better understand and memorize facts and their relationships to each other. When you review your chart after the lecture or activity, you remember the thoughts about analyzing, organizing, and comparing the notes you had written. Retention and recall are vastly improved every time you revisit the chart.

5. Charts can be used to create an overview of an entire lesson, unit, or course. Aligning the summarized key points of large chunks of the lesson into rows and columns makes a great study guide for students. The chart is comprehensive and provides students with the big picture, further reinforcing memory and understanding.

Disadvantages Of Charting

As with the other note-taking methods, charting has its disadvantages.

1. Some lessons contain data that may be juxtaposed with each other because they are unrelated. Useful headings and categories may be difficult to identify. Data elements may not be capable of comparison, thus situating them in a chart may not be meaningful.

2. You must prepare the chart ahead of time. Therefore, you must have advanced knowledge of the lesson or subject. When there is no occasion to read ahead or gain access to information about the activity, you might not be able to prepare a proper chart for taking down notes.

3. Some details may not fit in chart categories. Typically, this situation requires you to set up additional columns to accommodate the new details. But when the additional column categories do not apply to the other row entries, then you will have columns with single entries for a single row. The outcome defeats the purpose of having a chart.

4. Some details cannot be summarized into concise points because they require explanation. Realistically, they could not be accommodated into chart boxes in a way that makes sense, such as when the contiguous information is short and self-explanatory.

5. The physical size of the cells or boxes may just be too limited to contain substantial notes, so you may have to select a method such as outlining or sentence method.

When To Chart And What Chart Type To Use

The advantages and disadvantages imply that there will be circumstances when charting will be favorable and other times when it won't. For instance, if the lecture or material has a clear outline, you can use the categories of information to create a chart and use it for note-taking. Chart 2 above has column headings that directly refer to the headings in our chapters (e.g., how to use, advantages, disadvantages, and when to use).

Another clue is when direct comparisons can be made among elements in the information gathered. The subjects of comparison can form the row labels, while the criteria for their comparison can comprise the column labels, or vice-versa. The boxes where the subjects and criteria coincide will contain the details of the notes.

You may also use charting when details are easily compressed into concise forms. But when the notes require a great deal of elaboration, you should explore other forms of note-taking. If you still prefer the convenience of charting, you may vary the type of chart you are using to tailor it to the lesson you are taking down. You can use a T-chart (Chart 4), a Venn diagram (Charts 5 and 6), or a flowchart (Chart 7). These types of charts enhance how we compare information or the relationships between topics.

Based on its format, the T-chart compares two different but related kinds of events or ideas. The name of this special kind of chart comes from the lines drawn across the page in preparation for note-taking. The two things being compared are written on the horizontal line at the top, while either side of the vertical line lists the comparative differences between the two things. This format makes it easier for students to remember how two related things may be similar or different from each other.

T-Chart

Writers use a t-chart to plan a comparison
chapter for their informational text.

Make a t-chart below to compare to parts of your
topic/subtopic.

Wet or Dry?
Heading

Dry Dog Food	Wet Dog Food
-It is easy to store -It never needs refrigeration -It comes in a bag or box -Helps keep your dog's teeth clean -It is inexpensive -You can buy a large bag and it will last a really long time	- It needs refrigeration after opening -It comes only in a can -Most dogs love it -It makes some dogs sick -It can cost a lot -It comes in a lot of different flavors

Chart 4: The T-Chart [5]

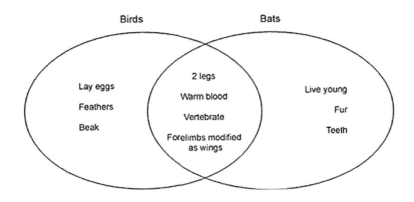

Chart 5: The Venn Diagram [6]

The Venn diagram is another special type of chart. Its purpose is similar to the T-chart, which is to compare the characteristics of two or more items. The number of items compared determines the number of circles used. See a five-circle Venn diagram below.

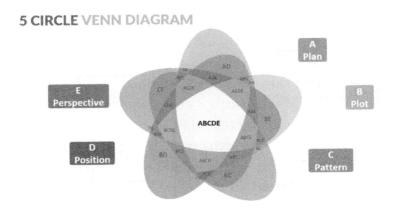

Chart 6: Five-circle Venn diagram [7]

The plurality of items compared is the advantage the Venn diagram holds over the T-chart. Comparisons are made in the overlaps of the circles over each other, where the similarities are situated. The differences (or the characteristics unique to the item) are situated in the parts of the circle that do not overlap. This is a great way to visualize similarities and differences from a comprehensive perspective. It aids both understanding and memorization.

The flowchart shown in Chart 7 departs from the purpose served by T-charts and Venn diagrams. Flowcharts visually represent processes; they illustrate how procedures are done. The components in a flowchart are shaped depending on their function − whether they are terminals, steps, decisions, documents, and so forth. They are linked by arrows that indicate the sequence of activities or the direction of data flow, depending on what the flowchart is supposed to describe.

Notice that charts and mind maps share two attributes: they employ graphic elements and organize information. They are included in a set of tools called graphic organizers. Mind maps and simple charts are classification graphic organizers since they describe the attributes of things. Flowcharts, cycle maps, and timelines are counted among sequence graphic organizers, while Venn diagrams and T-charts are called compare and contrast graphic organizers.[8]They each visually depict relationships between things. They are also useful for organizing notes.

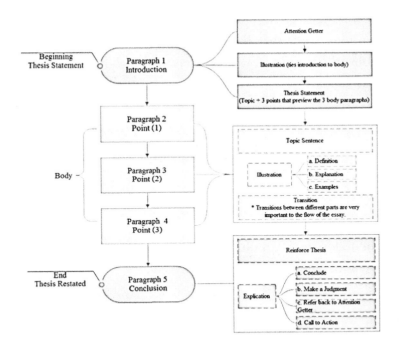

Chart 7: Flowchart [9]

Action Steps

Here is a simple exercise to gain some experience charting notes. Recall the action steps suggested in Chapter 3 where we discussed the outlining method of taking notes. The exercise should have resulted in an outline of items available either in a grocery store or restaurant menu. Take this outline, and create a chart outline based on its contents. The following steps are suggested to start you off in the right direction.

1. Note that the outline format likely has items in its main headings and the items' descriptive categories in its subheadings. These would likely form good column and row labels. Draw your horizontal and vertical lines accordingly.

2. Some of the lower-level entries could likely be classified under two or more of these categories. If some of these entries are classified under column and row labels that intersect, write them in the boxes at which these rows and columns intersect.

The following is an illustration of what the resulting chart may look like.

Selling Prices of Food Containers

Brand	Size by Volume Contents			
	1 Liter	2 Liters	3 Liters	4 Liters
Rubbermaid	$4.00	$8.00	$11.99	$15.99
Vtopmart	$4.89	$9.77	$14.66	$19.54
Dwellza	$7.47	$14.94	$22.41	$29.88

3. The foregoing is just one example. You may select the dimensions you prefer to include in the chart. In this

sample which regards information from the grocery store dry items, the column headings pertained to the items' sizes by volume and the row labels identified the items' brand. The specific detail entered into the cells were the prices of the items. At one glance, you can compare the prices of similar items.

Moving On

Standardized note-taking has greatly benefitted the field of medical care and treatment, as this chapter's opening story suggests. Technical data and complicated instructions can be simplified through chart formats, such as flowcharts used in computer science. Notes that are similarly compressed and recorded in charts can make their study and recall easier for students. However, the structure and brevity of chart notes may not be applicable for notes that need to be elaborated. The next chapter will describe a method by which notes of this type can be better accommodated.

Key Takeaways

- The charting method uses charts to condense and organize notes. A chart is a set of vertical and horizontal lines that divide the page into columns and rows. The notes are written concisely to fit into the cells where columns and rows intersect.

- The first step in charting is to identify the topics and categories that will comprise the column and row labels. Draw the vertical and horizontal lines to accommodate these labels. Then write down the headings and labels, and fill in the concise notes in each cell.

- The advantages of charting include recording the notes in a more compressed form, facilitating the analysis, understanding, and recall of the notes, and affording a comprehensive view of the entire lesson.

- Charting may not be applicable in all instances. Some lessons may not have categories that can be charted. Still, other lessons may resist being abbreviated or compressed, and therefore are not susceptible to charting.

- There are other types of charts, such as T-charts and Venn diagrams, that may be better suited to certain circumstances regarding note-taking. There are other techniques classified as graphic organizers that students may use for note-taking.

7

THE CORNELL METHOD - NOTE, CUE, AND SUMMARIZE

Remember Students A, B, C, D, and E? If they sound familiar but you can't quite place them, they were the memorable characters in the anecdote that opened Chapter 5. More specifically, they were the students who quoted words from my lecture when I suspected them of cheating in an exam. They happened to take down my lecture almost word for word, suggesting they used the sentence note-taking method. When they produced their notes and explained how they memorized them, they sufficiently justified how they came up with their exam answers. They did nothing wrong, they did not cheat, and so they deserved a good grade.

The story does not end there, however. As a teacher, I am obligated to teach my students. That means ensuring that they assimilate our class lessons in such a way that they can apply them fruitfully throughout their lives. Rote memorization does not do that. The students probably forgot the lines they memorized right after the exam.

In the anecdote, I said that I gave my five students all A's. I did, but not immediately. I told them to sit down and write, off the top of their head, what my statement meant. I asked them to paraphrase it and express its meaning in their own words. A good five minutes passed before I received the first answer and eight minutes before the last. The students spent the time reflecting on the statement to arrive at its meaning. Their answers were pretty good and, in some cases, even more profound than my memorized notes.

This experience underscores the difference between taking notes like a stenographer and learning from your notes like a good student. The raw notes need analysis, organization, review, and recall. The Cornell Method, more than any of the other note-taking methods, is the process that best ensures the student internalizes the lesson conveyed by the activity.

Defining The Cornell Method

The Cornell Method of note-taking is a "method of recording, organizing, and using the notes you take in class or from your textbook and readings." [1]Developed at Cornell University by Education Professor Walter Pauk in the 1950s,[2] it has stood the test of time and boasts a great success record. The Cornell Method incorporates not only the information you note down from lectures and texts but also records your comments, questions, and thoughts about these notes. It also includes a summary of your notes and integrates notes from other sources such as other lectures, textbooks, or readings. It is a great study tool to pass an exam successfully. [3]

Much like the charting method, you will need to prepare your note page ahead of the lecture, but this time according to a specific format. Each section of the Cornell chart is dedicated to a specific purpose.

How To Apply The Cornell Method

Perform the following steps: [4]

1. Divide the paper into three sections that include –

- A column on the right side of the page covering approximately 70% of the width.
- A smaller column on the left side of the page covering the remaining 30%.
- A short row at the bottom of the page.

2. The column on the right is used for lecture or text notes.

- Record your notes during the lecture as you normally would, and review them after the class to add in any missed information.

3. The column on the left is the "cue" column.

- Record questions here based on the main ideas in the lecture notes.
- Test your understanding by covering the lecture notes and answering the questions in the cue column.

4. The bottom section is used for a summary of the notes on that page.

Check out the following figure to see what the page looks like when it is divided into sections. Notice how the column widths are given in terms of inches rather than in terms of the percentage of the total width. The figure assumes that the width of the note page is the standard 8.5 inches across. If we calculate 70% and 30% of this page width, the results come close to 6 and 2.5 inches respectively. Giving the proportions in terms of percentages makes it easier for us to divide pages exceeding the standard size. Note that the length of the page does not affect the summary section's height and width. It is always measured 2 inches from the bottom since this section will contain only a summary of the page contents.

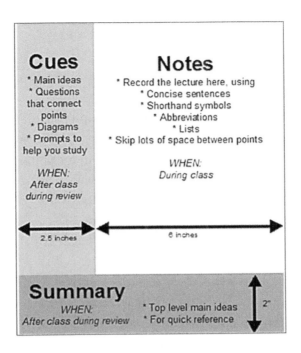

The Cornell Method format [5]

Let's go over what each section should contain.

The Notes Column

In the column on the right, which occupies the largest part of the page, you will take down notes as you listen to the lecturer, read a textbook, or gather information from whatever source. This is the only space you will write on during the lecture or reading when you capture the information. Remember the following:

- Use a writing style that is concise and abbreviated.
- Listen attentively and use your own words to paraphrase what you hear.
- Write in phrases rather than complete sentences.
- Use bullet points or lists wherever applicable.
- As with outlining, you could use indentation to show the relationship between ideas.
- Change pen colors to signify a change in concept.
- Know what to write; distinguish between important and trivial information.
- Note important cues from the lecturer: "This is important," "This may be included in the test," or repeated information, and highlight or underscore these in your notes.
- Indicate the teachers' formatting or note-taking requirements in this column, such as line spacing and font, outline style, graphs, diagrams, etc.

The Cues Column

The column on the left is the cues column, and it is filled after the lecture and while you review the notes you have taken.

- Write down the purpose of the lecture, reading, or source of information. If this is not immediately evident, write down what you think it is.

- Write questions that connect to or are answered by the key ideas in the notes on the right side. The questions should be of a higher level and must interact more profoundly with the key ideas.

- You may collaborate with your peers or colleagues to compare and enhance your notes as you review and revise them.

- Address any remaining points of confusion, and if necessary, add questions on the left side that you may want to ask the teacher or your peers. After you find the answers, add this to the right side (the Notes column) opposite the corresponding question on the left after the discussion.

The Summary

Write the summary after the lecture and the questions written down on the left. The summary is the synthesis of what you have learned from the lesson after you have analyzed and interacted with the notes you have taken.

- When writing the summary, address the essential questions in the Cues column, using the notes in the Notes column to support your answer.

- Combine the main ideas to better internalize the lessons learned.

Now that we're acquainted with the Cornell Method and its format, let's take a look at an actual page with notes written according to the method.

Example Of The Cornell Method

The sample page below shows the cues section with the heading "Questions/Main Ideas" and the notes and summary sections. It also has peripheral sections at the topmost portion that identify the topic and other details (name, class, period, date). These are useful additions to improve documentation of the activity. You will also note that the summary did not quite fit the page, so spillover notes (plus cues and summary) may appear on the next page.

Topic: Short Story Elements	Name: _____
	Class: English
	Period: 6
	Date: _____

Questions/Main Ideas	Notes
What is the definition of plot?	plot: events that take place in a story
	- exposition: beginning, intro(char, setting, etc.)
	- rising action: building up the climax; filled w/suspense tension
	- climax: turning point of story; decision of fate
	- falling action: events that lead to resolution, release of tension
	- resolution: conclusion/the end; conflict is resolved
	* conflicts: person vs person - btwn 2 people
	person vs nature - nat. disasters
	person vs society - mainstream society
	person vs self - w/in soul, heart, mind
	person vs supernatural - supernat. entity
Take note:	A good story has more than one conflict!
What are the different types of characters?	Static (flat): a character who's personality does not change throughout the story regardless of occurances
	Dynamic (round): a character who's personality changes throughout the story ➤ beliefs, morals, attitude, views, etc.
What is the definition/ purpose of theme?	Theme: moral message or overall point of the story
	- author creates the theme
	it's purpose to enlighten/educate/inform
	- meaningful enough to be applied into readers life
	- cleanse/purge your heart/soul/mind/spirit
What defines setting?	Setting: the description, time (era) of which the story takes place
	geographical location, historical time period, social setting
Summary: We're re-learning the elements of a short story. We went over the different types of conflict. We also reviewed the 2 types of characters: static and dynamic. I'd say the main character of

Sample of notes using the Cornell Method [6]

Advantages Of The Cornell Method

The method's two-column format provides space not only for recording the lecture notes but also for organizing and reviewing them. The cues section is a space for questions and insights that may cross your mind while you record the notes. The summary at the bottom makes the review handy and efficient. In effect, the Cornell method allows for organizing notes on multiple levels.

Writing the cues and summary on the same page as the notes provides an excellent tool for review and memorization. The notes portion contains the information from the lecture, while the cues section holds the musings and questions that pop up in the student's minds as they listen to the lecture. The summary is a recapitulation of the notes in the student's own words. The cues and summary are one degree away from the original material and incorporate the student's thinking. The Cornell method, therefore, encourages and guides learning. It documents the thought process and compels the student to assimilate the knowledge conveyed by the notes.

Disadvantages Of The Cornell Method

This method requires you to closely follow the lecture and focus your attention closely as it is being delivered. Then after the lecture, you must conduct the review immediately while the lecture is still fresh in your mind, and fill the column at the left and the space at the bottom with their appropriate content. If they are left for a much later time, the insights and questions you had in your mind might be forgotten, diminishing the usefulness of this method.

You may also have noticed that assigning space for the cues and summary columns limits the space for the note-taking column, particularly if you are using a standard-sized notepad. You may want to use a large-sized notepad and assign a larger width for capturing notes than the 30%-70% recommended proportion. A tickler will not work for the Cornell format.

When The Cornell Method May Be Suitable

It would be great to master this note-taking method because of the help it provides in analyzing, organizing, reviewing, and remembering the lesson. You can also adopt this method when rewriting notes gathered using the other methods, particularly sentence notes. After the activity, you will have more time and opportunity to mull over the lesson and condense it to its essentials. Your condensed notes could go into the Cornell "notes" section. The addition of cues/questions and a summary would enhance these notes.

There are occasions when the Cornell method may not be helpful. This style discourages writing long sentences. Some materials cannot be compressed or truncated into their short form. Passages from literary pieces or legal statements that are quoted verbatim are examples of notes that should not be abridged.

Overall, the Cornell method may enable students to write their notes and learn from them at a faster rate. However, academic studies have not formed a strong consensus about the effectiveness of the Cornell method in helping students improve their scholastic performance. A study by Quintus, Borr, Duffield, Napoleon, and Welch [7] found that there was no difference in student performance between those who used the Cornell strategy and others who used another method. Another study, authored by Akintunde, [8]found that Cornell note-takers outperformed students who used the Outline and Verbatim methods, while Outline note-takers did better than students who used Verbatim.

The academic studies that agreed or differed in their conclusion had diverse population samples, methodologies, and analytical statistics. Therefore, it is understandable that on these bases, they did not arrive at the same results. Students' academic performance, after all, depends on many factors, but mainly on the students themselves. The Cornell method is a systematic note-taking strategy that may help some students perform better if it suits their learning styles.

Action Steps

To perform this exercise, you will need an information source that is delivered in real-time, such as a lecture in class or raw notes you may have gathered without much organization. If you performed the action steps for Chapter 5, you have a set of notes in sentences. This is a good example of raw notes because it was written directly from a real-time source without undergoing much restatement or restructuring.

From the sentence-method notes, rewrite the information using the Cornell method. Be guided by the following steps.

1. As you reread the sentence notes, distinguish between the main ideas and the supporting or peripheral points. Rewrite them in the notes section, using compression,

indentation, or bullet formatting as you deem appropriate, to reflect the relationships among the ideas.

2. After you have completed the notes section, scan over the results and record any questions, insights, or reflections that come to mind in the cues column at the left. These comprise your thoughts about the notes. They are, effectively, what you have learned from the lecture, and extend into what you still wish to learn based on the questions you asked.

3. The final step is to write down two or three statements to summarize the notes and cues. These go into the summary section at the bottom of the paper. The purpose is not to restate everything, but to record the overarching concept to aid in the review and recall of the lesson.

Go back and read over your notes, cues, and summary. This being the first time, you may wish to refine what you had previously written. As you get accustomed to the Cornell method, you will quickly assimilate the lecture more profoundly and gain the most benefit out of it.

Moving On

The five students and I mutually learned from our shared experience. Although it began unpleasantly with a misunderstanding, the encounter helped us break new ground in our teacher-student relationship. The students grew in their appreciation of the need to assimilate the lesson and not merely memorize it. I gained insight into how teachers could better deliver the lesson to aid in this assimilation. In the following chapter, we will discover some pointers by which students and teachers can enhance interaction better for productive note-taking and learning.

Key Takeaways

- The Cornell method is a mode of recording, organizing, and using the notes taken from lectures, textbook readings, class discussions, and other academic activities.
- To prepare for taking notes using Cornell, divide the note page into three areas – the notes section, the cues section, and the summary section. Each section functions as a tool to record and learn from the activity.
- The notes column occupies the largest part of the page. It is where the notes from the activity are written down, as the activity is being conducted together with important instructions from the lecturer.
- The cues column occupies a two-inch margin at the left of the notes column. This is filled after the activity and contains the questions, insights, and main ideas derived from the activity notes.
- The summary section is also filled out after the activity. This is where you encapsulate the important points contained in the notes and cues.

8

HOW STUDENTS AND TEACHERS CAN IMPROVE NOTE-TAKING

G ene had taught in institutions of higher learning for more than two decades, mostly in courses involving mathematical calculations – physics, electronics, finance, and operations management. These subjects require a lot of board work for the equations and calculations that accompany the lecture. In his early years, Gene would breeze through his lectures with the enthusiasm of a sage imparting wisdom. He would fill the blackboard with formulas, derivations, and solutions to problems. The students would be dutifully bent over their notes, scribbling furiously, copying what was on the board.

Then, running out of blackboard space at the right, Gene would absent-mindedly reach for the eraser and make a grand sweep over the left side of the board. Suddenly, a multitude of voices would erupt in protest:

"Professor, NNNOOOOOOOOOOOOOO!!!"

The panicked outcry would shock Gene out of his lecture hypnosis and call his attention back to the students. "Wait, prof, we're not yet done copying!" With this realization, he would try to painstakingly restore the board notes he had just obliterated. "Uh-huh. Okay, kids, finish copying, quickly please," he would murmur beneath his breath. By the time he could reclaim the blackboard, he would have lost his train of thought.

Good thing the class reacted before the lecture proceeded. Had they been more withdrawn or intimidated, Gene would have gone ahead with his lecture, unaware that he had lost his connection with them. In class, lecturers should give as much attention to the students as they devote to the lecture. Note-taking effectiveness is a two-way street. Both parties should observe certain guidelines to ensure the smooth flow of information. There are no hard and fast rules, but academic researchers have unearthed a goldmine of information to suggest what steps we may take.

What Is The Function Of Note-Taking?

Before we can address the question of how to enhance the effectiveness of note-taking, we must understand the purpose that note-taking serves. There are two principal functions served by taking notes: (1) recording information and (2) promoting reflection.[1]

Recording information includes simple memory aids such as diaries or grocery lists. These notes serve as an external memory medium from which details are expected to be recalled at a later date.

Promoting reflection is something more subtle and profound. It involves a range of intellectual processes we may not realize we are doing, such as weighing options, resolving issues, making decisions, or solving mathematical problems. In this sense, notes are a way of coding information in a way that relieves mnemonic processes to help us develop a solution.[2]

Note-taking can be divided into two broad classifications – linear and non-linear styles. Linear styles follow the conventional written text format, where words and statements are sequentially written. Students commonly take notes according to the linear style. On the other hand, the non-linear style uses graphical representations, such as the method of mind mapping we discussed in Chapter 4. This style allows the notes to be organized in an unconventional yet systematic fashion, according to the student's preference. All graphic organizers, such as charts and graphs used to contain notes, are non-linear notes.

Students may adopt the linear, non-linear, or a combination of both styles. Whichever style they choose, the cognitive effort necessary for taking notes is the same. Therefore, the choice of style has little impact on content comprehension.[3] There may be a difference regarding effectiveness, however, because the non-linear styles facilitate a connection between ideas and concepts, thus enhancing deeper processing and long-term retention.[4]

Students become more systematic note-takers and, therefore, record lecture contents more accurately, yielding higher scores during tests.[5]

Why Take Notes By Hand?

In one academic study, a survey determined that out of ten note-takers, seven favored taking notes longhand with pen and paper (hard-copy note-taking), one preferred using an electronic device such as a laptop (soft-copy note-taking), and two indicated they equally used both hard and soft copy note-taking.[6]

When asked why most students preferred hard-copy note-taking, the overwhelming reason was that the use of devices (specifically laptops) was distracting. The distractions named included, in descending order, surfing the web, the sound of typing, games, online chatting, and email. From their answers, you could tell that nearly all of the distractions affected the note-takers themselves rather than the people adjacent to them (i.e., the sound of typing).

When asked about the benefits they got from their method, all respondents (both for hard and soft copy methods) named efficiency, retention, understanding class material, and organization. Students derived the same benefits from their preferred note-taking method.

Students allowed to take notes while listening to the teacher did better than those who only listened but were not allowed to take notes.[7]Students who wrote their notes by writing longhand achieved better scores than their peers who relied on notes provided by the teacher [8] or who used devices such as laptops.[9]

Indicators That Trigger Or Inhibit Note-Taking

Sometimes, without being instructed to, students instinctively pick up signals that certain parts of the lecture are important for notation, and others not so important. Boch and Piolat [10] arrived at a list of indicators for both. See if you agree with them.

Triggering indicators for note-taking include:

- Writing on the board (a very powerful indicator)
- "Dictation," or when the lecturer adopts slow and deliberate speech with a low vocal register
- A title of a section, a list, or the listing of information (often written on the board)
- Definitions and catchphrases (frequently noted even if not comprehended by the student)
- Words suggesting macro-planning organization and structure (expressions like "firstly"/ "secondly" or "primary"/"secondary")

Inhibiting indicators that signal exemption from note-taking include:

- Parentheses or asides (sequences that do not contribute to the organization of the conversation and that are intuitively perceived as introductory material, with a lower intentional register)

- Digressions, or interaction in class between the instructor and students (teachers' responses to students' questions) or even worse, between students
- Prosodic phenomena, which possess characteristics symmetrically opposite those of trigger indicators (faster delivery, higher vocal register) and commonly accompany the asides, parentheses, and digressions.
- Hesitations in speaking, which may signal that what is being said has not been planned by the instructor
- Certain paraverbal indicators, such as when the lecturer puts aside her notes or walks around the classroom (statistically, students pay less attention to what is being said at such times)

Why should we be aware of these indicators? Triggering indicators are noteworthy because they signal that important information is forthcoming. Lecturers can use these behaviors to prompt the students to prepare to take notes. Inhibiting indicators, on the other hand, signal to students that the information that follows is not part of the lecturer's planned material. Lecturers should avoid these indicators if the lesson they are currently conveying is important. Soft-spoken or monotonous speakers, or habitually loud speakers, might not be effective lecturers because they fail to take advantage of these indicators to signal what is important or unimportant to note down.

Insights For Students

As early as preschool, we were introduced to some rudimentary forms of note-taking. The teacher would write the letters of the alphabet on the board, and we would imitate the movements of her hand and replicate what she wrote on paper. Year after year, we treated note-taking as a skill we automatically adopted, but seldom did our teachers train us in its best practices. They probably assumed that we would find our way as we graduated from one year to the next.

Some teachers at the elementary level supervise their students' note-taking, teaching the basics of formatting (usually the outline method) and periodically grading their notebooks. But as students progress up the academic ladder, their lessons grow complicated, and their need for additional skills increases, but note-taking guidance fades away.

Many students never outgrow their early training of copying verbatim what the teacher writes (or says) even though they reach their secondary and tertiary levels. But studies have shown that taking notes verbatim or transcribing every word spoken by the lecturer, while more accurate, is maladaptive and superficial. It compels the student to dedicate too many cognitive resources to the small details while distracting from the bigger picture.

Learning becomes less effective during the note-taking process.[11]

Education experts tried to establish overall quality criteria for notes, but this proved to be highly variable. It so happens that the best judge of note quality is the user of the notes himself. Single-word notes that may not make sense to others could cue the creator of the note to recall a personal experience and its significance to the notes' topic.[12] This makes a lot of sense. When all is said and done, notes are only as effective for capture and recall as they relate to the individual note-taker. That is why we seldom really learn much from notes we copy from our classmates compared to what we learn from notes we take ourselves. Additionally, taking notes ourselves improves comprehension and makes us more independent learners, relying less on teachers and classmates.[13]

Suggestions For Students

1. Take notes in your own words. We call this taking generative notes. By casting notes in your own words, you actively think about the content of the lecture, digesting and comprehending it more thoroughly. Doing so facilitates the retrieval of information when reviewing the lecture. Paraphrasing has the advantage of avoiding unintentional plagiarism, but when you paraphrase, be sure of the accuracy of your notes.

2. Review early and often. Shortly after the lecture, review your notes and clarify any questions or uncertainties.

When the notes contain mathematical or other symbols (i.e., not syntactic), review them immediately and repeatedly because the incidence of errors in copying symbols is high. You may consult your peers, instructors, and the course materials, and resort to other means, preferably during the same day as the lecture. Space learning over several study sessions to foster long-term learning; do not cram.

3. Test yourself on your notes' contents by any relevant methodology. The Cornell method allows for this verification process. The purpose of testing yourself is to discover what you still may not have learned or retained from your notes. This practice will effectively improve your ability to recall the information when you need it.[14] 4. Choose your note-taking method carefully. Despite everything the academic journals say about which methods are more effective, remember that ultimately, the notes' effectiveness depends on their creator. What method works best for you? Would you prefer to draw charts or write statements, or maybe rely on one method to capture information and shift to another (or others) when reviewing and reorganizing?

4. Be careful of misperceptions during learning. Most importantly, avoid thinking that you know the lecture content better than you really do because this can lead to poor study habits.[15] This usually happens when the lessons deal with a topic about which much information (some misleading) circulates over popular channels such as social media. Gossip about unverified "fake news"

could also form some prejudgment about an issue without sufficient facts. Approach a lecture with an open mind, so that you may better analyze and judge the information received.

Insights For Instructors

The burden of good note-taking practices does not rest only on the note-takers. The lecturers and instructors should share the burden likewise. Instructors may speak too fast or fail to provide cues, rendering it practically impossible for their students to write good notes. They, therefore, obtain poor grades through no fault of their own. This does a disservice to the students and the teaching profession.

Giving students handouts in advance may give them a chance to review the material before the lecture. This helps them comprehend the lecture better when it is delivered, enabling them to better remember and assimilate the lesson into their long-term memory.[16] This is especially helpful for students with learning difficulties or cognitive impairments.[17]

Sometimes, instructors are pressured to finish their lessons in time, such that they tend to rush through their lectures. Through no fault of their own, students end up with incomplete notes. I remember one professor mentioning that the rate at which we speak is half the rate at which we think, but four times the speed at which we write. Özçakmak [18] affirmed that comprehension speed is faster than speaking speed, which in turn is faster than writing speed, and this fact plays an important role in note-taking.

Suggestions For Instructors

1. Motivate your students to take their notes in their own words. Encourage them to condense their notes and select important ideas. Explain to them how the best learning opportunity begins when notes are first taken, not reviewed or recalled. Comprehension and critical thinking expand as students listen to the lecture, and casting the notes in their own words helps them develop these skills. You could build these skills by punctuating your lecture with incisive and probing questions. Discourage them from repeating your own words; instead, ask them what these words mean to them.

2. Provide note-taking cues. Recall the two types of cues you can provide your students to help them enhance their note-taking, i.e., the importance cues and organizational cues. Importance cues can be written, oral, or nonverbal. Writing on the blackboard, posing a pre-question before a segment, and emphatic speech or body language (e.g., cradling your chin in your hand or raising your eyebrows), all alert the students that an important idea is being conveyed. Organizational cues may take the form of the outline of the topic discussed or preceding a segment with an introductory statement ("Next, we will examine the application of the theory of the firm"). Organization cues hint at the parts or details of the lecture being discussed.[19]

3. Supply your students with your lecture material before the lecture. Orient them toward important topics or ideas. The notes you provide may be complete or partial. Providing complete notes may make students lazy to pay attention in class since they are confident that the handouts are all they need. By providing partial notes, note-taking responsibilities are shared between the instructor and the student. You can provide blank spaces in the handouts to cue the students that something is missing that they should fill out during the class session.[20]

4. Pace your lecture. Many lectures and presentations, particularly those that are pre-recorded, proceed at such a rapid pace that students have difficulty keeping up. Remember to pause at strategic points during your lecture, and also provide opportunities for revision. It is also a good important cue to speak more slowly or repeat statements when coming to a key point. After completing a section, pause to clarify questions and allow your students to revise errors.[21] When it is appropriate, pause to make connections between the current and preceding lectures.[22] This reinforces reflection and recall.

5. Carefully consider your policy concerning laptops in the classroom. Laptops may be a helpful note-taking device, but they can potentially distract their users and other students during class. Despite this disadvantage, electronic devices may also facilitate quick access to information that could help their learning. Banning laptops in class may be extreme for institutions of higher learning and be met with resistance. Therefore, you may

want to consider designating an area of the classroom for those who use laptops, much as a "smoking area" is designated in a restaurant. The idea is to provide students the opportunity to use their devices if they so wish while ensuring the others an environment where they can listen to the lecture and take handwritten notes without distractions.

Action Steps

We take notes often and everywhere for a multitude of reasons, so we each assume responsibility for our own complete and accurate notes. But in a classroom setting, the lecturer or instructor should carry the lion's share of the burden to ensure their students have the opportunity to take good notes. Communication is the key.

Assume you are a lecturer. Try practicing the cues we have learned about while conversing with your subordinates at work, children at home, or similar individuals who rely on your instructive information.

1. When conveying something important, lower the register of your voice and speak more deliberately, emphasizing your words.

2. Precede your words by calling the attention of your listeners: "Okay, listen, this is important," or some similar prelude.

3. Pay attention to your body language. Attract your audience's attention to what you have to say by

maintaining eye contact, facing them squarely, and strategically using hand movements to demonstrate what you mean.

4. Pause briefly after saying something important and assess whether your listeners have absorbed its meaning. Repeat your message if the listeners appear unresponsive.

5. Ask your audience if they understood your message or if they have questions of their own: "Is this clear? Any questions?"

Moving On

Gene was an exceptional lecturer, but while he was oblivious to the note-writing needs of his students, he was ineffective for not accomplishing his goal of teaching them. Creating useful notes should be seen within the wider context of pedagogy, the method and practice of teaching. The teacher and student should work as a team: the teacher by distributing lecture notes or outlines in advance, pacing the lecture, and providing the appropriate cues, and the student by selecting the best note-taking method, drawing the most benefit out of the notes, and communicating to the lecturer to slow down, clarify, and elaborate.

Key Takeaways

- Note-taking serves two important functions: to record information and to promote students' reflection on the information gathered.
- The two note-taking styles are linear and non-linear. Linear is the conventional style that uses statements and phrases, while non-linear uses graphic organizers that are unconventional but systematic.
- More students prefer handwritten (hard-copy) note-taking, but a growing number are shifting to electronic (soft-copy) modes. Those who write longhand have a better comprehension of the notes on average, but ultimately, the note creator determines the effectiveness of the method chosen.
- Instructors convey both triggering and inhibiting indicators that cue the students regarding important and unimportant sections in the lecture.
- Research has revealed numerous insights and suggestions for both students and instructors to improve their note-taking experience.

AFTERWORD

Prehistoric art in the Pettakere Cave, Indonesia [1]

When did humans first feel the need to record their lives or aspects of them? The earliest known writings had been in early civilizations such as Egypt or China. But even before that, prehistoric people already felt the urge to leave their mark on the world they inhabited in the form of cave drawings.

The earliest cave art dates back to approximately 64,000 years ago. [2] The one shown above has been carbon-dated up to 40,000 years of age. [3] They showed hand stencils and figures of animals, or stick figures of people hunting, swimming, and going about their daily lives. Some archaeologists hypothesized that early humans did this to represent beauty, or to influence nature or the ancient gods.

For whatever reason prehistoric people set their marks on walls or caves, two things are for sure: the marks were meant to be permanent records of things thought to be important, and this became a tradition taught to succeeding generations. It is not a stretch of the imagination to say they are primitive peoples' early notes.

Today, tens of thousands of years later, we continue to take notes. The medium is different, as well as the symbols and codes, but the intention is the same – to create records that store information in a permanent external location that may be retrieved sometime in the future. But unlike our primitive ancestors, we use note-taking in a deliberate attempt to enhance our learning effectively. We experiment with media, styles, methods, and techniques, all towards one end: to improve learning. This is why we need to know the learning style that suits us most.

There are many things we have discussed in this book that you are already likely familiar with. The note-taking methods you had used in school would have at least included outlining, sentence, and charting. The chapters covering these topics should provide you with a comprehensive review and maybe some fresh insight to complement what you already know. Mind mapping and the Cornell method are relatively new methods that would have added to your knowledge and provided you with new note-taking skills that you could use in the future. The last chapter integrates past and current research on what students and instructors can do to improve the note-taking process. The knowledge you would glean from this chapter will be most valuable to you, whether you are performing the role of a student or instructor.

In parting, let us leave you with the following adage from Robert Pyle [4]:

"You can see that there is scarcely an observable fact unworthy of mention in your notes, and yet you could easily spend more time scribbling than watching, and that would defeat the purpose. So be selective, don't be compulsive, and enjoy your note-taking."

Do not forget that the world you are experiencing is what you seek to capture, and your notes can only approximate it. Keep your eyes, ears, and mind open, and condense the essence of what you see, hear, and think in your notes.

CONTINUING YOUR JOURNEY

 Those Who Keep Learning, Will Keep Rising In Life.

— CHARLIE MUNGER (BILLIONAIRE, INVESTOR, AND WARREN BUFFET'S BUSINESS PARTNER)

The most successful people in life are those who enjoy learning and asking questions, understanding themselves and the world around them.

In our Thinknetic newsletter we'll share with you our best thinking improvement tips and tricks to help you become even more successful in life.

It's 100% free and you can unsubscribe at any time.

Besides, you'll hear first about our new releases and get the chance to receive them for free or highly discounted.

As a bonus, you'll get our bestselling book *Critical Thinking In A Nutshell* & 2 thinking improvement sheets completely for free.

Go to thinknetic.net to sign up for free!

(Or simply scan the code with your camera)

THE TEAM BEHIND THINKNETIC

Michael Meisner, Founder and CEO

When Michael got into publishing books on Amazon, he found that his favorite topic - the thinking process and its results, is tackled in a much too complex and unengaging way. Thus, he set himself up to make his ideal a reality: books that are informative, entertaining, and can help people achieve success by thinking things through. This ideal became his passion and profession. He built a team of like-minded people and is in charge of the strategic part and brand orientation, as he continues to improve and extend his business.

Diana Spoiala, Publishing Manager

From idea to print, there is a process that involves research, outlining, writing, editing, and design. Diana oversees all stages of this process and ensures the quality of each book.

Claire M. Umali, Publishing Co-Manager

Crafting books is collaborative work, and keeping everyone on the same page is an essential task. Claire coordinates every member of the team involved in crafting Thinknetic's books, attending to queries and providing support wherever needed. In her free time, she writes reviews online and likes to bother her cats.

Dianna Aquino, Writer

The author has a doctorate and has taught in college and graduate school for 40 years. Outside the academe, she has had field experience in business management, engineering, law, finance, and marketing. She has been married for 37 years and has raised three children, now professionals in their own right. Her wealth of experience and academic foundation enable this book's grounded approach through straightforward explanations and everyday examples.

Alfonso E. Padilla, Content Editor

Mexican editor with a background in journalism. Alfonso takes pride in his curiosity and cares deeply about learning. True to his formation, he prioritizes solid research and sources when reviewing texts. His main tool for editing is the use of questions.

Sandra Agarrat, Language Editor

Sandra Wall Agarrat is an experienced freelance academic editor/proofreader, writer, and researcher. Sandra holds graduate degrees in Public Policy and

International Relations. Her portfolio of projects includes books, dissertations, theses, scholarly articles, and grant proposals.

Jezreel Arvin Iglesias, Researcher

Arvin is a young, self-driven freelance writer specializing in conversational blog-content writing. He is a quick learner and can adapt to different writing styles. Arvin has a wide range of experience with learning and writing about different niches. He incessantly looks for opportunities to expand his horizons and sharpen his skills.

Ralph Escarda, Layout Designer

Ralph completes our books' journey to getting published, making sure that every book is properly formatted. His love for books prevails in his artistic preoccupations. He is an avid reader of non-fictional books and an advocate of self-improvement through education. He dedicates his spare time to doing portraits and sports.

REFERENCES

1. Why Take Notes?

1. Adapted from Blackbourn, N. (2018, March 8). Why is note-taking important? Nick Blackbourn. https://nickblackbourn.com/blog/why-is-note-taking-important/
2. Muraina, M. B., Nyorere, I., Emana, I. E., & Olanrewaju, M. K. (2014). Impact of Note Taking and Study Habit on Academic Performance Among Selected Secondary School Students in Ibadan, Oyo State, Nigeria. *International Journal of Education and Research*, 2(6), 437-448.
3. Almaagbh, I. F.F. (2020). The Impact of Strategic Notetaking on EFL Learners' Academic Performance in Jordan. *International Journal of Higher Education*, 9(1), 249-255
4. Salame, I. I. & Thompson, A. (2020) Students' Views on Strategic Note-taking and Its Impact on Performance, Achievement, and Learning. *International Journal of Instruction*, 13(2), e-ISSN: 1308-1470
5. Ruggiero, V. R. (2012). *The Art Of Thinking: A Guide to Critical an2020d Creative Thought (10th ed.)*. New York, NY: Longman.
6. Murawski, L. M., EdD. (2014). Critical thinking in the classroom… and beyond. *Journal of Learning in Higher Education*, Vol. 10, Issue 1, Spring, 25-30.
7. Ruggiero, V. R. (2012). *The Art Of Thinking: A Guide to Critical and Creative Thought (10th ed.)*. New York, NY: Longman, 4.
8. Arum, R. & Roksa, J. (2011). *Academically Adrift – Limited Learning on College Campuses*. University of Chicago Press
9. Haber, J. (2020, March 2). It's Time to Get Serious About Teaching Critical Thinking. *Inside Higher ED*. https://www.insidehighered.com/views/2020/03/02/teaching-students-think-critically-opinion

2. Learning Styles And Note-Taking Methods

1. Krukov, Y. (2021). *Students and Teacher in the Classroom Near Brown Table* [Photograph]. Pexels. https://www.pexels.com/photo/students-and-teacher-in-the-classroom-near-brown-table-8197494/

2. Malvik, C. (2020, August 17). 4 Types of Learning Styles: How to Accommodate a Diverse Group of Students. *Rasmussen University*. https://www.rasmussen.edu/degrees/education/blog/types-of-learning-styles/

3. Malvik, C. (2020, August 17). 4 Types of Learning Styles: How to Accommodate a Diverse Group of Students. *Rasmussen University*. https://www.rasmussen.edu/degrees/education/blog/types-of-learning-styles/

4. See the VARK Official Website: https://vark-learn.com/

5. Sphero Team. (2020, December 8). 4 Types of Learning Styles: Explaining the VARK Model. *Sphero*. https://sphero.com/blogs/news/learning-styles-for-kids

6. Somji, R. (2018, April 17). Teaching Strategies for the 9 Different Learning Styles. *VirtualSpeech*. https://virtualspeech.com/blog/teaching-strategies-different-learning-styles

7. (2013, September 4). The Seven Learning Styles. *Inspire Education*. https://www.inspireeducation.net.au/blog/the-seven-learning-styles/

8. (2013, September 4). The Seven Learning Styles. *Inspire Education*. https://www.inspireeducation.net.au/blog/the-seven-learning-styles/

9. Chapman, A. An Introduction to Kolb's Learning Styles. *BusinessBalls*. https://www.businessballs.com/self-awareness/kolbs-learning-styles/

10. McLeod, S.A. (2017, October 24). Kolb's Learning Styles and Experiential Learning Cycle. *Simply Psychology*. https://www.simplypsychology.org/learning-kolb.html

11. McLeod, S.A. (2017, October 24). Kolb's Learning Styles and Experiential Learning Cycle. *Simply Psychology*. https://www.simplypsychology.org/learning-kolb.html

12. Kolb, A. Y., & Kolb, D. A. (2013). The Kolb Learning Style Inventory — Version 4.0: A Comprehensive Guide to the Theory, Psychometrics, Research on Validity and Educational Applications. *Experience Based Learning Systems Inc.*, 10.

13. Furey, W. (2020). The Stubborn Myth of Learning Styles: State teacher-license prep materials peddle a debunked theory. *Education Next*, 20(3), 8-12.

14. Adapted from McCombes, S. (2022, May 10). How to Write a Summary. *Scribbr*. https://www.scribbr.com/working-with-sources/how-to-summarize/

15. Merriam-Webster. (n.d.). Analyze. In *Merriam-Webster.com dictionary*. https://www.merriam-webster.com/dictionary/analyze

16. Li, Y., Medwell, J., Wray, D., Wang, L., & Liu, X. (2016). Learning Styles: A Review of Validity and Usefulness. *Journal of Education and Training Studies*, 4(10), 90-94.

17. JoanDragonfly. (2017, June 9). *Types of Learning Styles* [Illustration]. Flickr. https://flic.kr/p/UnmNA6

3. Outlining – Points And Hierarchy

1. See Public Domain Files Website: http://www.publicdomainfiles.com/

2. Triceratops, T-Rex, and Stegosaurus, from left to right.

3. (2017, October 19). Outline Notes: How to Use this Method for Better Note-Taking. *GoodNotes Blog.* https://medium.goodnotes.com/how-the-outline-note-taking-method-works-f0808ea2cbfa

4. Adapted from Hunter College. (2022). The Writing Process: Guidelines for Outlining. *Hunter College.* https://www.hunter.cuny.edu/rwc/handouts/the-writing-process-1/organization/Guidelines-For-Outlining

5. Adapted from Hunter College. (2022). The Writing Process: Guidelines for Outlining. *Hunter College.* https://www.hunter.cuny.edu/rwc/handouts/the-writing-process-1/organization/Guidelines-For-Outlining

6. Ratnayake, I. (2019). *Brown and Black Yorkshire Terrier Puppy* [Photograph]. Pexels. https://www.pexels.com/photo/brown-and-black-yorkshire-terrier-puppy-4084988/

7. Seongbin, I. (2010). *Black Russian Terrier and My Daughter* [Photograph]. Flickr. https://www.flickr.com/photos/59899594@N00/4910285146

8. GoodNotes. (2017, October 19). Outline Notes: How to Use this Method for Better Note-Taking. *GoodNotes Blog.* October 19, 2017. https://medium.goodnotes.com/how-the-outline-note-taking-method-works-f0808ea2cbfa

9. Watson, S. Fun with Outlines. No, Really. *Writing with Sharon Watson.* https://writingwithsharonwatson.com/outlines/

4. Mind Mapping - Creating Roads To Knowledge

1. Courtesy of Google Maps
2. Erdem, A. (2017). Mind Maps as a Lifelong Learning. *Universal Journal of Educational Research*, 5(12A), 1-7.
3. Buzan, T., & Buzan, B. (2007). *The Mind Map Book.* Edinburg, Englad: BBC Active.
4. Wickramasinghe, A., Widanapathirana, N., Kuruppu, O., Liyanage, I., & Karunathilake, I. (2008). Effectiveness of mind maps as a learning tool for medical students, *South East Asian Journal of Medical Education,* 1(1), 30-32.
5. Brinkmann, A. (2003). Graphical Knowledge Display – Mind Mapping and Concept Mapping as Efficient Tools in Mathematics Education. *Mathematics Education Review,* 16, 35-48.
6. The University of Adelaide. (2014). Mind Mapping, Writing Centre Learning Guide. *The University of Adelaide.*
7. Michalko, M. (2001). *Cracking Creativity: The Secrets of Creative Genius.* Berkley: California Ten Speed Press, 2001.
8. Adapted from Buzan, T. (2005). *Mind Map Handbook*, Great Britain: Thorsons.
9. The University of Adelaide. (2014). Mind Mapping, Writing Centre Learning Guide. *The University of Adelaide.*
10. The University of Adelaide. (2014). Mind Mapping, Writing Centre Learning Guide. *The University of Adelaide.*
11. Mahmud, I., Rawshon, S., & Md. Jahidur Rahman. (2011). Mind Map for Academic Writing: A Tool to Facilitate University Level Students. *International Journal of Educational Science and Research*, 1(1), 21-30.
12. Mahmud, I., Rawshon, S., & Md. Jahidur Rahman. (2011). Mind Map for Academic Writing: A Tool to Facilitate University Level Students. *International Journal of Educational Science and Research*, 1(1), 21-30.
13. Created using the EdrawMind Versatile Mind Mapping Tool.

5. Sentences – Explaining Whole Ideas

1. Tamm, S. (2021, December 11). "The Sentence Method of Note-Taking: A Quick Guide." *e-student.org.* https://e-student.org/sentence-note-taking-method/

2. Oxford Learners Dictionaries. (n.d.). Monolithic. In *OxfordLearnersDictionaries.com dictionary*. https://www.oxfordlearnersdictionaries.com/us/definition/english/monolithic?q=monolithic
3. Promonotes. (2022). The sentence note taking method. *Promonotes.* https://promonotes.de/zdaniowa-metoda-sporzadzania-notatek/

6. Charting Method – Sorting Things Out

1. Correll, R. (2020, July 13). Nurse Charting 101. *Berxi.* https://www.berxi.com/resources/articles/nurse-charting-101/#what-are-the-different-types-of-nurse-charting
2. (2022, July 10). Charting Method of Notetaking. *Ms. Liew's Class.* https://msliewsclass.weebly.com/charting-method.html
3. Common Goal Systems, Inc. (2022).Online Gradebook. *Teacher Ease.* https://www.teacherease.com/online-gradebook.aspx
4. Peltier, J. (2005, June 10). *That "inefficient" manner of arranging the data is actually very flexible, enabling you to filter and pivot the data, and it's pretty close to a way to display your data.* [Reply to *Plotting 4 dimensions in a chart*]. Excel Forum. https://www.excelforum.com/excel-charting-and-pivots/377941-plotting-4-dimensions-in-a-chart.html
5. (2022, July 10). Charting Method of Notetaking. *Ms. Liew's Class.* https://msliewsclass.weebly.com/charting-method.html
6. (2022, July 10). Charting Method of Notetaking. *Ms. Liew's Class.* https://msliewsclass.weebly.com/charting-method.html
7. PowerSlides, Inc. (2022). *PowerSlides.* https://powerslides.com/powerpoint-diagrams/venn-diagram-templates/5-circle-venn-diagram/
8. Lynch, A. (2021, July 20). What is a Graphic Organizer? *Wondershare.* https://www.edrawsoft.com/what-is-graphic-organizer.html
9. Lynch, A. (2021, July 20). What is a Graphic Organizer? *Wondershare.* https://www.edrawsoft.com/what-is-graphic-organizer.html

7. The Cornell Method - Note, Cue, And Summarize

1. McLaughlin Library, University of Guelph. (2022, June 30). *Study Effectively*. https://guides.lib.uoguelph.ca/StudyEffectively/CornellMethod#s-lg-box-15768703
2. Pauk, W., & Owens, R. J. Q. (2010). "Chapter 10, The Cornell System: Take Effective Notes," *How to Study in College*, 10th edition. Cengage Learning.
3. McLaughlin Library, University of Guelph. (2022, June 30). *Study Effectively*. https://guides.lib.uoguelph.ca/StudyEffectively/CornellMethod#s-lg-box-15768703
4. Adapted from McLaughlin Library, University of Guelph. (2022, June 30). *Study Effectively*. https://guides.lib.uoguelph.ca/StudyEffectively/CornellMethod#s-lg-box-15768703
5. Guhlin, M., (2018, September 1). Technotes. *Microsoft Tips and Tricks*. https://blog.tcea.org/cornell-note-taking-with-onenote/
6. Comprehension Strategies. (2022). Cornell Notes. *Comprehension Strategies*. http://comprehensionhart.weebly.com/cornell-notes.html
7. Quintus, L., Borr, M., Duffield, S., Napoleon, L. & Welch, A. (2012). The Impact of the Cornell Note-Taking on Students' Performance in a High Scholl Family and Consumer Sciences Class. *Journal of Family and Consumer Sciences Education*, 30(1):27-38.
8. Akintunde, O. O. (2013) Effects of Cornell, Verbatim, and Outline Note-Taking Strategies on Students' Retrieval of Lecture Information in Nigeria. *Journal of Education and Practice*, 4(25):67-73.

8. How Students And Teachers Can Improve Note-Taking

1. Boch, F. & Piolat, A. (2005). Note Taking and Learning: A Summary of Research. *The WAC Journal*, 16:101-113, DOI: 10.37514/WAC-J.2005.16.1.08
2. Boch, F. & Piolat, A. (2005). Note Taking and Learning: A Summary of Research. *The WAC Journal*, 16:101-113, DOI: 10.37514/WAC-J.2005.16.1.08
3. Friedman, M. C. (2014). *Notes on note-taking: Review of research and insights for students and instructors.* Harvard Initiative for Learning and Teaching, Harvard University.

4. Piolat, A., Olive, T., & Kellogg, R. T. (2005). Cognitive Effort during Note Taking. *Applied Cognitive Psychology*, 19(3), 291–312. https://doi.org/10.1002/acp.1086

5. Robin, A. L., Martello, J., Foxx, R. M., & Archable, C. (1977). Teaching note-taking skills to underachieving college students. *The Journal of Educational Research*, 71(2), 81–85. https://doi.org/10.1080/00220671.1977.10885042

6. Berkovatz, J., & De Guzman, E. (2011). The Evolution of Note Taking: A Study on Traditional Hard Copy Methods Vs The Emerging Soft Copy Method. Uses and Gratifications Final Narrative Project. San Jose State University.

7. Kiliçkaya, F., & Çokal-Karadaş, D. (2009). The Effect of Note-taking on University Students' Listening Comprehension of Lectures. *Kastamonu Education Journal*, 17 (1): 47-56.

8. Sridharan, M. Cornell Method – A method to take great notes. *Think Insights.* https://thinkinsights.net/consulting/cornell-method-great-notes/

9. Mueller, P. A., & Oppenheimer, D. M. (2014). The Pen is Mightier than the Keyboard: Advantages of Longhand over Laptop Note Taking. *Psychological Science*, 25(6). https://doi.org/10.1177/0956797614524581

10. Adapted from Boch, F. & Piolat, A. (2005). Note Taking and Learning: A Summary of Research. *The WAC Journal*, 16:101-113, DOI: 10.37514/WAC-J.2005.16.1.08

11. Kiewra, K. A., Colliot, T., & Lu, J. (2018). Note This: How to Improve Student Note Taking. *IDEA Paper #73.*

12. Friedman, M. C. (2014). *Notes on note-taking: Review of research and insights for students and instructors.* Harvard Initiative for Learning and Teaching, Harvard University.

13. Özçakmak, H. (2019). Impact of Note Taking During Reading and During Listening on Comprehension. *Academic Journals Educational Research and Reviews*, 14(16):580-589. https://doi.org/10.5897/ERR2019.3812

14. Friedman, M. C. (2014). *Notes on note-taking: Review of research and insights for students and instructors.* Harvard Initiative for Learning and Teaching, Harvard University.

15. Friedman, M. C. (2014). *Notes on note-taking: Review of research and insights for students and instructors.* Harvard Initiative for Learning and Teaching, Harvard University.

16. Boyle, J.R., & Rivera, T.Z. (2012). Note-Taking Techniques for Students with Disabilities: A Systematic Review of the Research. *Learning Disability Quarterly*, 35:131-143, https://doi.org/10.1177/0731948711435794

17. Friedman, M. C. (2014). *Notes on note-taking: Review of research and insights for students and instructors.* Harvard Initiative for Learning and Teaching, Harvard University.

18. Özçakmak, H. (2019). Impact of Note Taking During Reading and During Listening on Comprehension. *Academic Journals Educational Research and Reviews,* 14(16):580-589. https://doi.org/10.5897/ERR2019.3812

19. Kiewra, K. A., Colliot, T., & Lu, J. (2018). Note This: How to Improve Student Note Taking. *IDEA Paper #73.*

20. Kiewra, K. A., Colliot, T., & Lu, J. (2018). Note This: How to Improve Student Note Taking. *IDEA Paper #73.*

21. Kiewra, K. A., Colliot, T., & Lu, J. (2018). Note This: How to Improve Student Note Taking. *IDEA Paper #73.*

22. Friedman, M. C. (2014). *Notes on note-taking: Review of research and insights for students and instructors.* Harvard Initiative for Learning and Teaching, Harvard University.

Afterword

1. Cahyo. (2014). *Hand prints in Pettakere Cave at Leang-Leang Prehistoric Site, Maros* [Photograph]. Wikimedia Commons. https://commons.wikimedia.org/wiki/File:Hands_in_Pettakere_Cave.jpg

2. Hoffmann, D.L., Pike, A.W., García-Diez, M., Pettitt, P.B., & Zilhão, J. (2016). Methods for U-series dating of CaCO3 crusts associated with Palaeolithic cave art and application to Iberian sites. *Quaternary Geochronology,* 36: 104–119. https://doi.org/10.1016/j.quageo.2016.07.004

3. Lew, J.. (2018, October 24). 10 Incredible Ancient Cave Paintings. *ThoughtCo.* https://www.thoughtco.com/best-ancient-cave-paintings-4869319

4. Pyle, R. M. (1992). *Handbook for Butterfly Watchers,* ed. Houghton Mifflin Harcourt.

DISCLAIMER

The information contained in this book and its components is meant to serve as a comprehensive collection of strategies that the author of this book has done research about. Summaries, strategies, tips and tricks are only recommendations by the author, and reading this book will not guarantee that one's results will exactly mirror the author's results.

The author of this book has made all reasonable efforts to provide current and accurate information for the readers of this book. The author and their associates will not be held liable for any unintentional errors or omissions that may be found.

The material in the book may include information by third parties. Third party materials are comprised of opinions expressed by their owners. As such, the author of this book does not assume responsibility or liability for any third party material or opinion.

The publication of third party material does not constitute the author's guarantee of any information, products, services, or opinions contained within third party material. Use of third party material does not guarantee that your results will mirror our results. Publication of such third party material is simply a recommendation and expression of the author's own opinion of that material.

Whether because of the progression of the Internet, or the unforeseen changes in company policy and editorial submission guidelines, what is stated as fact at the time of this writing may become outdated or inapplicable later.

Printed in Great Britain
by Amazon

19837824R00092